No Ball Games Allowed

40 talks to reach and teach your teens

Darren Trainer

Trafford rev. 01/06/2012

 www.trafford.com

North America & international
toll-free: 1 888 232 4444 (USA & Canada)
phone: 250 383 6864 ✦ fax: 812 355 4082

Acknowledgements

Thank you to everyone who has supported and encouraged me to keep going and to see this book finally arrive in print.

Thanks to those who helped with verses, photos, offering feedback and ideas.

Special thanks go to Ingrid Morris and my wife Adele for many hours of editing, without them the book wouldn't have been completed. So a huge thank you to both of you.

For Erin, Ben and Megan

Preface

There are many excellent books which provide youth leaders with an outline of a programme or an idea for a talk but I had never seen one which gave leaders a structure and skeleton content on which to build. There can be an expectation that young leaders will know how to talk to youth groups and often no training is provided. My aim is to help leaders with ideas, structure and content for speaking to youth groups.

On the front cover is a sign that I pass everyday and the title of the book came from seeing the shadow of the cross formed by the sun on the sign. When I was a boy the sign saying "no ball games allowed" was the worst that you could come across. They usually appeared in an area of grass perfect for football or golf but they prevented me from having fun. Many young people see the cross as something that is against any kind of fun and the equivalent of "no ball games allowed". They see it as a book full of rules and "thou must nots".

Jesus tells us that He came to bring life, freedom and joy. I hope that as you use these talks your group will see the cross as a symbol of love and not the equivalent of a "no ball games allowed" sign which spoils their fun. May you reach out to your youth group to show the hope and joy that can be found in a relationship with Jesus Christ through the cross.

Contents

Introduction

As I have written this book the most frequently asked question has been "who is the book for?" The short answer would be everybody!

The longer answer is that it is for those involved with young people and especially those who talk to youth groups. In this sense the book gives forty talks that any leader can read and use. The talks are designed to be read in an "as you would say it" format, but I fully expect that most leaders will add or subtract from the skeleton text.

This book is aimed at those who perhaps are new to youth work or those who struggle to put a talk together. Hopefully the structure of the talks alone will give help in this area. But even if you are an experienced youth leader, there are times when a new idea is most welcome!

Every talk is aimed at **teaching** those who are Christians already and **reaching** out to those who are not yet Christians. The aim is to challenge and encourage young people to think of who God is, what He has done and what He can do in their lives. Each talk opens with a story or a general thought on the subject and then teaches those who are Christians and reaches out to those who are not yet Christians.

Some of the talks include personal stories about me or my children – I would envisage that these stories could still be used although not in the first person or replaced with something similar from your own experience. These talks are not a script to be read word for word, but rather an outline of what can be said to illustrate a point or to make young people challenge their beliefs and perceptions. However teenagers are interested in YOUR life so it would be better to use your own illustrations and develop the habit of noting down events and ideas as they occur.

Are these talks a substitute for daily notes? No. However as each talk is independent of the others they could be read as individual encouragements or challenges to Christian faith.

Finally the book was written for youth workers like me; endeavouring to lead young Christians, speak of our faith to those who have no faith and yet all the while striving to live out the very messages we deliver each week. Yes, it's for you too. Whilst writing the book I was continually challenged with the paradox of what I was typing and how I was living out my faith.

May you know the truth of what we speak of and may the young people that you work with see the reality of Christ in you (and me!)

The New International Version of the Bible has been used for quotes unless otherwise stated but I would recommend the website www.biblegateway.com as an excellent resource for viewing alternative versions.

Top tips

Who is your audience?

Anyone from twelve upwards, it may be a youth group, sports club, study group, a new Christians group or nurture group.

What interests them?

Try to keep the talk relevant to them and the things that are important, difficult or fun for them.

Get their attention

You may have five minutes or maybe ten but the key is getting and keeping their attention. You may be speaking after the most energetic of nights or at the end of a long day. Grab their attention in that first minute!

Timing

If you say you'll be five minutes, be five minutes. Think of what you want to say and then stick to it.

Complicated or simple?

Every talk can be as simple or as complicated as you want it to be. Maybe you want to source additional verses or maybe you feel that one verse is enough for your group. That's absolutely fine. You are the best judge of the needs of your group. You could show music or movie clips, build a whole programme around it or add questions to discuss in study groups.

Challenging them

In any talk you will want to encourage and challenge. Be specific in the challenge; what action would you like to see them take as a result? Is it to invite a friend or pray about something?

Presenting

Remember that for the five or ten minutes that you are talking, it's up to you to hold their attention. Try and look at all areas of the room so that no part of the group feels left out. Be visual! You are allowed to move and move your hands!

Using humour

One of the best ways of getting attention or keeping attention is humour. It can be part of the story or a way in which you deal with interruptions. Just be careful to balance the humour with the content.

Audience participation

Some talks have questions or activities that require an individual or the group to participate. This can be a great attention grabber but can be a distraction if they become too noisy or don't quite carry it out as asked!

PowerPoint

If you are comfortable with PowerPoint this can be a great resource. If you are using verses or images this allows everyone to see them whilst you are talking. If you are not comfortable or it's not possible then that's ok – just make sure that you are holding their attention. The opposite is true if you use PowerPoint – this can become the centre of attention rather than something you refer to when needed.

Being prepared

It may only be five or ten minutes but the key to any talk is being prepared. Prepare, practice and pray. Prepare what you want to say, practice it so that you are confident in the timing and content. Finally pray, because you may be the speaker but it is God who does the challenging and the encouraging!

Sharing

If you want to reach young people or help them to grow in their faith then they need to see you modelling this faith. So when you talk it is helpful to share with them the reality of your faith – the highs and the lows (where appropriate).

Relationship is the key

Some conversations can only happen when trust and rapport have been established and this emphasises the need to build strong relationships with your group. So take time to be available for questions or conversation after you have spoken. You talk to five or one hundred young people from the front of a room but conversations are 1 to 1.

The best team in the world

Outline

Was there anything special about the 12 disciples? Collectively they changed the face of the world as they formed and grew the early church after Jesus' death. Were they the greatest team the world has ever seen?

Opening

Which is the greatest team the world has ever seen?

Well that's impossible to answer because there will be so many options and it would be hard to compare teams from different areas, for example *(you could get them to shout out a few suggestions here or give them some clues to guess these ones)*

- Brazil football team 1970
- Manchester United 2008
- The team of people who worked with Bill Gates on Microsoft
- The team of people that designed the first space shuttle
- Is it the Beatles because they were the biggest pop group?

The next question would be what do we mean by a team? Is it a group of people working together towards a common goal or purpose? Or a group of people who need each other to achieve something?

Jesus describes the church as a body made up of many parts that are reliant on the others to perform and work as designed. The disciples came from very different walks of life. For example; fishermen, tax collector and zealot (extremist) to name a few. Somehow they worked together to achieve something quite remarkable.

TEAM – Together Everyone Achieves More

Teach

How is church for you? How are your Christian friendships? What are you currently doing in your Christian service that takes more than just you?

It's very rare in the Bible to read of disciples doing things on their own, Jesus sends two of them to find the donkey tied up (Matthew 21:1-2). Was this to verify what happened? Was it for their protection? Was it to support one another?

In terms of church and families, we are not designed to be alone, we are created and designed to be part of a team, to be part of a community, to be part of something that is bigger than us.

Think about the disciples for a moment, the different personalities and backgrounds – Matthew the tax collector, probably clever (hated by Jews), Peter the rugged fisherman who just tells it like it is!

Do you ever doubt your qualities, what you bring to the "team" church? Don't! If the disciples teach

> Jesus can and does use **anyone** who is prepared to trust in Him.

us anything it's that Jesus can and does use **anyone** who is prepared to trust in Him. You see being a Christian and serving God is about God working through you. All God needs is a willing heart and someone who says "yes". God will do amazing things through people who are committed to serving Him.

 Reach

So what exactly did the 12 achieve? There is a verse that speaks of someone telling the authorities, just leave these men alone because if it's not of God then it will come to nothing but if it is of God then do not oppose it. (Acts 5:38-39)

2000 years on and the church of Jesus Christ continues to grow, it is of God, for God and from God. We can look at 12 men who came from different backgrounds and worked together to share the gospel of Jesus but without the 13th man they would have failed. You see every great team has a great coach, a leader, someone that the team looks to for guidance and inspiration.

The disciples were a frightened, sad lot as they waited in locked rooms after Jesus' death. Their leader had gone and the team was in trouble. But the coach comes back from the dead for one team talk and tells them that He will "send another" coach to be with them and that this coach will always be with them. This coach comforts us when things go wrong, instructs us in the way we should play and corrects us when we play badly! He is the Holy Spirit.

Jesus knows your potential; He doesn't just see what you are but what you can be!

Jesus knows your potential; He doesn't just see what you are but what you can be. In terms of victory, Jesus tells us that He has won the battle/match/game on our behalf before it was even played. Imagine the biggest competition you have ever entered and knowing beforehand that victory was already yours!

Jesus has won in your battle with sin and death; He asks you today "Do you want to be on the winning team?" The prize is there for you but you need to play His way, you need to live for Him. The disciples may be the best team ever but there is no doubt that the best coach the world has ever seen is Jesus.

What a difference a day makes

Outline

To look at how the world changed in 24 hours through Jesus' death on the cross. Some people say a week is a long time in politics or football, but the world was changed forever one day in Bethlehem and then again one day in Jerusalem.

Opening

Jack Bauer of 24 fame, is a man who has days that no-one else has! The premise of the show is that each episode lasts one hour and there are 24 episodes. We follow Jack in "real time" throughout very eventful days! (Except has anyone noticed that he never sleeps, eats or visits the loo?)

In each episode Jack has various major challenges that involve saving his family, saving the President and saving America from terrorists. We follow Jack through the struggles of one amazing twenty four hour period and wonder how he can turn it around and save the day. He often faces huge dilemmas like: do I save the President or do I save my daughter? He never sleeps, never stops, never eats during the day that we are with him and yet still has the strength to take on everyone and everything. What a guy!!

The incredible thing is that each episode changes the world in some way. What would have happened if the President had been assassinated, or a biological attack had taken place?

It's only a TV show....but we forget about two 24 hour periods that have changed the world forever and they were for real!

One day in Bethlehem a baby was born to a young couple, the mother was Mary and the husband was Joseph (but he was not the father) the father was God. On that day, in that stable, God came to earth in the person of Jesus.

On another day in Jerusalem approximately 33 years later, Jesus willingly died on a cross despite never having done anything wrong in His life.

Two days that changed the world.

 **Teach**

There are two questions here for you in the light of these thoughts;

1. How has your life changed as a result of these two days/events?

2. Do you go into each day believing that God can do amazing things in just one day?

• • •

If it doesn't change you and me then how can we convince others?

• • •

It's very easy for Christians to speak about the fact that Jesus came and lived on earth and that He died on the cross. But – and it's a big but – if our daily lives do not reflect anything of this then what does that say to those around us? We can argue that Jesus' life, death and resurrection changed the world, but if it doesn't change you and me then how can we convince others?

Jack Bauer often had to convince others of the reality of the threat facing them or the country, unless he was utterly convinced of the danger it was unlikely he would be able to persuade others that it existed. Are you convinced of the danger that non-Christian friends are in?

Do we think that God changed the world on those two days but does not change things now? They happened 2000 years ago. Do we believe that God can do something amazing with our lives today? Do I believe that God can do amazing things in and through me? God is still doing amazing things in the lives of Christians every day – answering prayers, healing people, bringing people/events together in unbelievable ways. I have prayed for the seemingly impossible and then watched it happen. So what do all the examples above have in common? …..Christians who have trusted in the Lord and believe He can do more than we can ask or imagine. (Ephesians 3:20)

Do we believe that God can do something amazing with our lives today?

 **Reach**

What has been the most significant day in your life? Why?

Have there been days that changed your life? Sometimes for good, other times not. I remember specific days when I was told of the deaths of grandparents and in my early teens these days changed my life in some way. Other big days were exam results arriving, memorable events at school or sport that bring pleasure (or pain!)

Have any of these genuinely changed your life forever?

Think about our daily lives, we make decisions all day and we try to do our best for ourselves whilst not hurting others. We battle with what we want for ourselves against the pressure of helping others. We want it all now but know we should wait. We want happiness every day but know that's not realistic. We want healthy lives but know that without exception we all will die.

The two days 2000 years ago dealt with all these areas and more. Jesus comes as God in the form of a man and lives with human emotion, temptation, fear etc. Jesus then dies on a cross and in doing so addresses the failings of the world. He says that if you trust in me you will never die, you will go to Heaven where there will be peace, joy, no death and no battle between right and wrong.

There will be a day when every Christian will gather in Heaven. The world as we know it will have come to an end and our lives in Heaven will have begun.

What a day that will be, will you be there?

Three questions everyone needs to answer!

Outline

To look at the fundamentals of Christianity – who was Jesus, what do we need to do in order to be a Christian and what's involved in being a Christian?

Opening

I want to look at three questions with you, one that Jesus asked, one that someone asked Jesus and one that we need to answer almost daily.

1. Jesus asked Peter *"Who do you say that I am?"* (Mark 8:29) This came at the end of a discussion concerning who people said Jesus was and where He may be from. Jesus asks the direct question to one of His disciples (almost saying never mind who they say I am) *"Who do **you** say that I am?"*

First and foremost, you need to decide who Jesus was. History has ample evidence that Jesus lived, indeed our calendar is set in terms of BC and AD – before Christ and Anno Domini – the year of our Lord. In other words the date that you write each day declares the significance of Jesus Christ. There are historical documents that speak of Jesus and our Bible is made up of different accounts of Jesus' ministry by those who knew Him or obtained firsthand accounts of what took place.

Jesus was God's Son, our Saviour and our first need is to believe that this is true.

2. Our second question was asked by a rich young man who had it all and believed that he knew it all – yet he asked Jesus *"Teacher, what do I need to do to inherit eternal life?"* (Mark 10:17)

"Teacher" in those days would be the equivalent of Rabbi, Minister, Pastor, Man of God etc. It was an acknowledgement that Jesus was a man of spiritual worth, leadership and worthy of listening to. Today this question would be like asking "Minister, Youth Pastor, what do I need to do to be a Christian?"

There are lots of answers to this one, some people will say A, B, C – Accept, Believe, Confess. But I just want you to think of one thing – faith. You see the question, "how do I become a Christian" or "how do I get to Heaven" involves one key thing – faith. It's not about you; it's not about what you have done, what you will do or who you are.

It is a decision that should change your life, your priorities and your heart.

In fact it's about God. It's about a faith in Him that says I trust that you love me, that you died for me and that my faith in you alone is enough. Not fancy words, not fancy prayers – just a faith that says I want to trust and believe in you God. This isn't a decision you just make with your head, it's a life decision. It is a decision that should change your life, your priorities and your heart.

3. Our third question is the one that I said we could ask ourselves daily (or God Himself may ask us). What will you do with Jesus?

You see the choice here is this, walk with Him or walk away from Him. Trust Him or reject Him?

For some this will be a decision that you face for the first time. For some others you may be saying I trusted Jesus years ago and that's enough – well yes and no!

 Teach

Some Christians often sit quite comfortably through talks like this thinking, "well I tick all the boxes, I believe Jesus is God, I believe I am going to Heaven so I'm sorted."

Let me be fairly blunt – that's not what the Christian faith is about! Yes it starts with a decision but it doesn't end there. The Christian faith is a journey NOT a prayer prayed once and then we continue on as before. God demands and deserves more. To acknowledge that Jesus is the Son of God, to believe that you are right with God through Jesus Christ and yet to avoid Him or deny Him a place in your life each day, is wrong.

So when you look again at that question "What will you do with Jesus?" ask yourself – "what am I doing with Jesus, what do I need to start doing and who do I need to talk to about my faith" By answering these questions then you will start to really walk with Jesus and the journey will start to take shape.

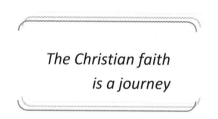

The Christian faith is a journey

 Reach

Those first two questions are really the key. Who is He? What do you need to do?

Firstly, you can't really deny that Jesus lived, He did. History tells us He did; it also tells us that He was crucified. This was not unique as thousands were crucified during this period of history. So we know He lived, we know that hundreds, even thousands witnessed miracles. And we know that hundreds were said to have seen Him alive again after His death. So the first question is key "Who do **you** say that I am?"

Secondly, being a Christian begins with admitting our need of God's forgiveness and the belief that Jesus was who He claimed to be – the Son of God. Once you believe this and have faith in Him as God, then your journey begins because your walk with God is not about you but instead it's about the Son of God who loved you.

Is it all in your genes?

Outline

Does where we come from affect who and what we are? To consider what we love and what we will do for the things that we love. If we love God, what are we doing for Him?

Opening

In the book of Matthew in Chapter 1 there is an outline of the descendents of Jesus and it includes some very unlikely people. Firstly it is surprising that this family tree includes women (given it was written in a male dominated culture) and then there is the fact that one of these women was a prostitute! So although Jesus was the Son of God, here we see His "human" family tree and it tells us of kings, adulterers and prostitutes!

I recently found out that my great grandfather played football for Celtic; he was known as the "great Johnny McMaster". Given my love of football it was interesting to find out that he played the same position as me (although probably a bit better) and played for Celtic over 200 times, winning trophies and medals.

However the most interesting fact I found was that Johnny was playing for Celtic when World War I broke out and this interrupted his playing career. However in 1917 when on leave from service Johnny was staying at barracks in Edinburgh, all servicemen were instructed not to use public transport, trains etc. so Johnny had to walk everywhere. The time of his leave coincided with Christmas and New Year – and the "Old Firm Derby"! Rangers v Celtic! This is played in Glasgow, 40 miles from Edinburgh.

Such was my great grandfather's love for Celtic and football; he walked from Edinburgh to Glasgow to play in that New Year's Day game! Forty miles for a game of football! He was on leave from fighting the most brutal war in history and yet rather than take it easy he chose to walk all these miles to play for the team he loved.

Teach

Here is the challenge – we are told that as Christians, we are children of God, so do people see this in us? Is there a family resemblance? If there is, then we will love the things that God loves and our behaviour will show this. Do we resemble Christ? Jesus was loving, forgiving, kind, meek, faithful and strong. He clearly demonstrated His love for us.

When did you last demonstrate your love for God, when did you last walk forty miles for God? When we love someone or something our actions give it away! This is true when we have a girlfriend/boyfriend where we want to talk to them often. We want to spend as much time with them as possible, we buy them gifts, we want to please them and we want to know that they love us too. Jesus wants to spend time with you, give you the best, and show you His love.

So as Christians we love God. We want to please God, we want to spend time with God and we want to serve God... or do we? We know the love in the heart of God because we are His children so then let me ask you Christian – what's in your heart?

It is a well used phrase that "people don't care what we know until they know that we care". Sometimes that will involve being a friend to someone going through a hard time, it may be taking the first step to settle an ongoing argument, or it could be doing something in your spare time that is solely for the purpose of helping others. Jesus himself said that He didn't come to be served but rather to serve.

 Reach

We all love something, football, clothes, music, gadgets etc. We will save money and sacrifice things in order to get what we want. My great grandfather wanted to play that day, he was determined to play that day, he loved the club and the game so much that he walked the forty miles to play.

> *God loved you and me so much that He was prepared to send His Son to earth and let Him die*

The most famous verse in the Bible says *"For God so loved the world that He gave His only Son, so that whoever believes in Him would not perish but might have eternal life"* John 3:16. Forget about walking 40 miles; forget about going without McDonalds or a CD in order to get what you really want. God loved you and me so much that He was prepared to send His Son to earth and let Him die in order for you and me to know how much He loves us. If He was prepared to let Jesus die to demonstrate His love for us then how much must He love us?

When Johnny McMaster arrived at Celtic park for that game, he was given a shirt and he went out as part of the Celtic team. He was picked and then he played.

Picture Jesus in Heaven with the team sheet in His hand, your name is not on it and He asks you, "Do you want to be on the winning side?"

Jesus loves you; by trusting in Him you join Him in His victory over sin and death and you "play" forever in His team both here on earth and in Heaven. When you trust in Him you become a child of God, part of God's family.

Past, present or future?

Outline

To challenge young people with the reality of the Bible for today and for the future. Do they see it as a book of history, written two thousand years ago or is it real to them today?

Opening

The Bible has approximately forty authors – from the time of Abraham all the way through to John who wrote his letters in approx 98 A.D.

It contains prophecies (predictions) written hundreds of years in advance predicting events that would occur (and did occur). Some of these relate to Jesus' birth, where He would come from, how He would die and what would happen to Him. All of these prophecies were written hundreds of years before Jesus was born.

So how do you feel when people talk about the Bible? Do you think "yeah yeah that was two thousand years ago" or maybe you think "yeah I'm a Christian but Heaven is sixty years away for me".

So what if I gave you a time machine and told you that you could go anywhere in history and meet anyone who has ever lived; what if I told you that you could witness one event in history.

What would you choose?

Who would you want to meet? *(You could ask for some suggestions here or give some of your own)*

I wonder if meeting this person or witnessing what you saw would change you as a person.

Would events of the past or the life of someone who lived in the past have an impact on you today and how you lived from now on?

Teach

Sometimes as Christians we are seen as being two thousand years in the past or fifty years ahead of ourselves. That's not how God intends it to be....being a Christian is about today!

Is that what your Christian life has become? Have you made a decision of faith about a man who lived two thousand years ago and then trusted that you will be in Heaven in sixty, seventy years time?

A time machine is interesting to think about because so many interesting things have happened and so many great men and women have lived through history. But you are called to live your life for God today. God has a desire to be real to you today/tonight not in 50 years time! In fact God wants to be as real to you today as He was to Moses, David and those disciples as they established the church.

So how can God be real to you today?

- Do you pray? Do you read your Bible or do Bible notes?
- When did you last do something that was scary for God? For example, invite someone to your youth group, tell them about your faith, or serve God somehow, somewhere.
- When did you last exercise faith in your Christian life?

For God to be real today we need to involve Him in our lives today and we need to do things now that deepen our faith in Him.

Reach

The time machine game is always fun. Imagine looking over Rome when the Roman Empire was at its peak. Or imagine the Wild West in the times of the cavalry and Indians or maybe you would only go back a few years and meet Elvis or Marilyn Munroe.

What if you could go back and watch Jesus walk about in Galilee or Jerusalem. I wonder what you would think and do after watching Him "come alive" rather than just hear about Him as another character from history.

What would you say if I told you that Jesus is as real today as He was then and rather than you watching Him, Jesus actually watches over you!

Jesus cares for you, every single part of you and every second that you are alive.

● ● ●

He cares what you think
He cares what you do
He cares who your pals are
He cares what you say
He cares how you behave
He cares who you go out with
He cares what you watch on TV

● ● ●

Yes, He is the God of two thousand years ago and beyond. Yes, He is the God of Heaven and eternity. Today this same God is saying to you – I want to be real to you and to walk with you today.

Where were you?

Outline

To look at the big events in the last ten years that have had an impact on the world. Do we remember where we were when we first heard the news of these events? Do big events change history? Has the birth and death of Jesus Christ changed the world?

Opening

The past ten years has seen some huge events that have changed lives, countries or the world in some way. *(You could get your group to guess the year the following occurred)*

- Concorde crashes — July 2000
- Twin Towers attack — September 2001
- Queen Mother dies — March 2002
- Saddam captured — December 2003
- Tsunami disaster — December 2004
- Pope dies — April 2005
- London bombings — July 2005
- Obama elected — November 2008
- Michael Jackson dies — June 2009
- William and Kate's wedding — April 2011

For some of these stories you may remember the day you watched them on the news or where you were when you heard about them. Whilst some of the stories might not be important to you, but they will be to others.

What would you think has been the biggest news story ever?
Has it been a discovery of some kind? (Maybe of penicillin or man on the moon)
Has it been an event? (Maybe the start or end of a World War)

We maybe only imagine that news started when TV was invented or when newspapers started being printed. But what is the most significant thing that has ever happened in all of history?

In every century there have been significant events, battles, tragedies, nations conquering nations, religious authorities squashing the beliefs of others, disease, discovery of new lands and new nations beginning.

What has been the most significant news story of your life? The story that stays in your memory – where and when you saw it on the news or read it in the paper. Did it change your life for a day, a week, a month or forever?

Teach

This story of Jesus that we believe in is often referred to as the "Good News" or the "greatest story ever told". Our world is dominated by bad news. The next time you watch the news, listen to what the stories are about – bad news. That's why they have the "and finally" item as a way of finishing the half hour news on a positive or nice story.

> The story of Jesus is the most amazing story the world has ever or will ever hear.

The story of Jesus is the most amazing story the world has ever or will ever hear. Our job as Christians is to tell that story. If you are a Christian then the fact that you are a Christian tells the story – you are a Christian, a follower of Christ, a believer in Jesus Christ. Your life should tell the story of a life changed by God, a life turned around by God's love and forgiveness. So, when people look at you and me, do they see good news?

We should be the "and finally" item, the positive thing that stands out amidst the bad news of the world. We believe that God knows us, loves us, forgives us, lives in us and has rescued us so that one day He will take us to be with Him in Heaven forever. Does that excite you? Do you want to share that kind of news with others?

It's only when we believe, truly believe, that we have good news that we will start to share it with others.

Reach

Where are you today? Not physically, but spiritually. As you hear this message of God's love, where are you?

As Jesus died on the cross, there were people at the foot of the cross, people standing at a distance watching, people walking by shouting insults and laughing. Where are you? Are you at a distance thinking "who cares!" Perhaps you are like the people nearer the cross watching and listening but not yet believing in Jesus.

The man at the foot of the cross was not a Christian, he was a Roman soldier. We would imagine him to be tough and battle hardened. He would have seen many crucifixions in his time and yet this one was different. Whilst some spat, some shouted and others stood at a distance. It was the man nearest the cross who said *"Surely this was a righteous man"* Matthew 23:46.

> *Jesus' death can bring you forgiveness and the chance to start afresh.*

The best place to be is near the cross because then we see Jesus as He really is. When we see Jesus as He is, it changes us forever. That's the Good News; Jesus' death can bring you forgiveness and the chance to start afresh.

What is Love?

Outline

To look at the pressures on young people regarding sex. God is love and God created sexual relationships, so is love all about sex? To explain the three different uses of the word love in the Bible.

Opening

Take a look at any magazine – irrespective if it's for boys or girls, men or women – and ask yourself what is the cover all about? *(You could have some examples to show at this point)*

In a word, sex.

Every male magazine will have a semi-nude female on the cover, giving the message that she is desirable and available and the magazine sells itself to you on that basis. Likewise for girls, if it's not a hot guy then it's someone like Cheryl Cole *(or equivalent)* telling you it's easy to look like her and that you should look like her. She will probably be telling you that she has "7 secret beauty tips" that will make you look just like her!

Really? 2 litres of water a day, lots of sleep, a smoothie for breakfast and the occasional chocolate bar (but not after dinner) and you could be just like Cheryl!

So what are the key messages portrayed here?
Guys – your girlfriend should be as desirable as the cover girl.
Girls – if you don't look and dress like Cheryl, then you should, because that's what the boys want.

So both sexes think that the good looking ones are all in a relationship, having a great time together and if you aren't "at it" then you should be!!

What a lot of rubbish!

The hype around sex and celebrity status has been driven to encourage the sale of magazines, papers and television ratings. This creates a pressure in adults and teenagers alike. So our self esteem can be built around our desirability and sex life. That's not how God planned it.

God is love, God created us, He created sex, so sex is not bad or rude. In fact when God created man and woman He was pleased with all He had created. So sex is not wrong.

When we say God is love, we need to understand that in the Bible love can mean 3 different things – or to put it another way – there are 3 different types of love.

Philos – a love that relates to friendship and companionship

Eros – a sexual love, the root of our word erotic, an intimate love

Agape – the love that God has for us, an eternal, unconditional kind of love

Sadly when we hear people talk about love, they generally link it to sex. So let's look at this type of love first and let's first examine the lie that is fed most often to teenagers; everyone is doing it and they are all good at it!

Everyone ISN'T doing it and everyone ISN'T great at it!

Eros love – a sexual, intimate love

The Bible is very clear that sex is a natural act and is an expression of love BUT it was designed to take place between a husband and wife. The Bible talks of a man leaving his parents, (getting married) and then "being one" with his wife. This oneness relates to them as a couple being one in spirit and also being one in the physical sense.

It's important to be very clear that God thinks sex is good, normal and part of a healthy marriage – that's what He designed it for. Likewise the physical attraction that you feel toward the opposite sex is a natural God given feeling. We are designed to be attracted by each other's looks, personality, sense of humour etc. But sex and the expression of love in this way is meant to be enjoyed in marriage not on the basis of lust or desire created by magazines, music videos, TV and peer pressure.

sex should be an expression of intimate love within a marriage

When I was ten I wanted to drive my dad's car just like him. I knew what to do – start the car, put the car in 1st gear, handbrake off, accelerate and steer. Easy! The truth was I knew what to do but I wasn't ready to drive until I was able to put the knowledge and awareness together. Everyone who has sat through sexual health education at school knows the how to, magazines tell you the what to do but the Bible tells us the when and why.

The Bible tells us that sex should be an expression of intimate love within a marriage where both people are committed to one another and also God's designed method of reproduction.

So what about the other two types of love described in the Bible?

18

Philos love – the love a friend has for another

A man once asked Jesus *"What is the greatest commandment?"* Jesus replied, *"Love the Lord your God with all your heart, mind and soul and love your neighbour as yourself."* (Matthew 19:19) In the Bible, your neighbour can be interpreted as anyone that you come across (friend, neighbour, family, person at school, person on the bus, person on TV or internet on the other side of the world)

1 Corinthians 13:4-7 tells us what love is meant to look like. It's often read at weddings as people make promises and declare their love for one another but these qualities are meant to be apparent in all that we do.

"Love is patient, love is kind. It does not envy, it does not boast, it is not proud. It is not rude, it is not self-seeking, it is not easily angered, it keeps no record of wrongs. Love does not delight in evil but rejoices with the truth. It always protects, always trusts, always hopes, always perseveres."

So when you think about your friends and the kind of friend that God wants you to be, then look again at this list because we all want and need to have friends like this.

Agape love – the unconditional love of God

Everything that we have looked at in terms of magazines flies in the face of this kind of love. The images and articles promote a thought process of – I love you because you are sexy, you are willing, you are available, being with you will make me look good, feel good...

...such is His amazing, unconditional love for you.

God says I love you...
There is no "because", there is no "if".

God created you, knows you and wants you to enjoy a relationship with Him. This relationship will involve an intimacy that can only be had with God, a friendship that is unique and a love for Him that is based on an appreciation of God's amazing love for you.

A verse in the Bible says *"greater love has no man than this, that he lay down his life for his friends"* (John 15:13). Do you love anyone enough to die for them? God did! Jesus, God's Son chose to die for you, such is His amazing, unconditional love for you.

It's not a love you find in a magazine. It's not based on fake promises or lust or guilt. No, it's a love so amazing that it changes lives and changes people.

God loves you. How will you respond to His love?

It's good to talk

Outline

How do we communicate every day? As a society, we are addicted to it and most of us use many methods of communicating on a daily basis. But what about the simplest and most amazing communication of them all – prayer. Do we pray?

Opening

It's incredible how many ways there are to "talk" to one another. We are constantly using so many ways to communicate with friends, family, work. How many can you think of?

Phone – Landline
Mobile phone
Text
Fax
Computer/Laptop – email
Blackberry/iPhone
MSN
Facebook
Twitter
Skype
Sign language
Writing (card or letter)
Talking face to face

Today we can talk to anyone, anywhere in the world at anytime. I have a friend in Australia and I can talk to him as I am starting my day and he is ending his – I say talk but I type on my laptop and within two seconds the words appear on his phone or his laptop in Australia.

Everyone has a mobile and everyone wants the newest, coolest mobile and when you get it, what's the first thing you do? Text your friends to tell them you have a new phone! Soon the novelty wears off and it's just another phone.

So how amazing is it to you that you can talk to God?

Teach

Have you been taking communication with God for granted? Is it like the old mobile phone, you know it's there but the excitement has gone?

Maybe we have lost sight of what we are doing when we pray. Think again about what you are doing; the God of all creation, the God of Heaven, is listening to all that you are saying. Not only is He listening, but He has also promised to answer you too!

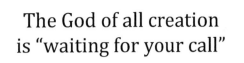

The God of all creation is "waiting for your call"

Here is an amazing thought; the God of all creation is "waiting for your call". He wants to hear your thoughts, issues, concerns, about the people who are important to you, everything! Unlike some of your friends, He's never engaged or not in or has no money left to reply.

We are told to *"cast your cares on Him, because He cares for you"* (Psalm 55:22). We are also promised that *"if my people.......will humble themselves and pray...... then I will....hear"* (2 Chronicles 7:14).

Mobile phones have changed communication forever but answered prayer changes lives for eternity.

How often do we miss out because we do not pray? We are amazed by the latest fancy technology (Skype, iPhones, ...) and yet by simply talking or even silently thinking to God – we are able to communicate with the God who created everything. He sits wanting you to talk to Him. Mobile phones have changed communication forever but answered prayer changes lives for eternity.

So how long do we spend talking to God and how long do we spend on texting, msn etc? Let's make speaking to God a priority this week!

 Reach

Isn't it funny, I am telling you about talking to God and you perhaps think I am mad? What if I told you that in my hand I have the mobile number of Beyonce and David Beckham? What if I said I could give these numbers to one person and they could make one call to them? You may be giving the impression that you are unimpressed but I know that everyone would secretly love the chance to talk to one or both of them – think of it, to have the personal contact details of Beyonce and Becks would be incredible. What would you ask? What would you say? Would you be screaming on the phone? Would one call be enough? You have seen them and heard them on TV but suddenly you could be talking to them.

What I am talking to you about today is the personal contact details of God. God wants a relationship with you and like all relationships it starts with a conversation. God knows all about you but wants you to get to know Him. You have the means and the opportunity but the question is will you use it? God sits in Heaven hoping that you will speak to Him and start a new relationship with Him.

God hears our prayers whether they are said quietly in our head or whether they are spoken out loud. He isn't interested in big words or fancy language, He just wants to hear what's in your heart. Go on, speak to Him today.

What's the most famous quote ever?

 Outline

To look afresh at the most well known verse in the Bible, what does it actually mean? Can we learn something of its importance by looking at other well known quotes?

Opening

What are the most famous quotes of all and why?

- "One small step for man, one giant leap for mankind" Neil Armstrong
- "I have a dream..." Martin Luther King
- "They think it's all over, it is now" Kenneth Wolstenholme
- "Some people think football is a matter of life and death. I don't like that attitude. I can assure them it's much more important than that" Bill Shankly
- "We will fight them on the beaches, we will never surrender." Winston Churchill
- "Never leave till tomorrow that which you can do today" Benjamin Franklin
- "To err is human, to forgive is divine" Alexander Pope
- "Knowledge is power" Francis Bacon
- "For God so loved the world that He gave His one and only Son, that whosoever believes in Him shall not perish but have eternal life" John 3:16

Some quotes have become so famous and so well quoted because they are associated with major events, major figures in history or because they seem to succinctly say things that are of great importance.

Neil Armstrong: The first man on the moon and a huge event in the history of mankind. Armstrong's quote makes you picture the figure of him jumping off the ladder onto the surface of the moon as millions watched on TV and gasped that a moon landing had been achieved.

Martin Luther King: A speech of great significance as he championed the rights of African Americans for equality with "whites" in America. A dream that was to become a reality. (Although some may say it's still ongoing)

Winston Churchill: In the midst of World War II when Britain feared invasion and probable defeat from Germany, Churchill delivers this speech that many believe changed the course of the war. He motivates everyone for a surge against the enemy and inspires such belief that Hitler thinks again about invading Britain.

Francis Bacon: A quote still used in business as a means of telling people that by acquiring knowledge and information they would be in a position of superiority or advantage over others.

Bill Shankly: What a ridiculous thing to say about football! But many who shout and scream at TVs every night would make you think that it's true! In reality we know it's only a game.
Kenneth Wolstenholme: Although as a Scotsman it pains me to admit it, England did win the World Cup in 1966 (it's very rarely mentioned!) This quote is spoken as Geoff Hurst scores that 4th goal and people run onto the pitch to celebrate.

 Reach & Teach

John 3:16: The most famous Bible verse of them all. A verse that in many ways sums up the 66 books and 1189 chapters in one sentence. In many ways it contains all of the reasons why these other quotes are special:

- A first for mankind (like the moon landing) as God becomes man and sends His Son from Heaven to earth to show His love for mankind.

the Lord Jesus actually won the war for you and me

- A dream? God knew in advance all that would happen when He created this world and yet still loved us enough to let us do our own thing. It wasn't a surprise to God that we sinned or that Jesus had to die.

- A war? Absolutely! Jesus came to win the ultimate war, good vs. evil, God vs. devil, life vs. death, Heaven vs. hell. Churchill didn't shoot a gun or fight in the war but the Lord Jesus actually won the war for you and me.

- Now you have the knowledge! If you never knew before now, now you do: God loves you and Jesus died so that if you trust in Him and believe in Him, you will be forgiven and He will never leave you.

- A matter of life and death? Yes it is and the key word is "if". **If** you believe in Him **then** that eternal life, that forgiveness may be yours. But if you don't, then the eternal life will not be yours.

- *"It is finished!"* Jesus' last words on the cross. It's over, the war is won for those who trust in Jesus. Whilst the "game" i.e. life continues, the outcome has already been decided. When you trust in Jesus Christ and have faith in Him then the victory is assured. Your hope, your strength and your eternity is assured because you trust in Him.

> Your hope, your strength and your eternity is assured because you trust in Him.

"For God so loved the world that He gave His one and only Son, that whosoever believes in Him shall not perish but have eternal life" (John 3:16)

Words so amazing, so life changing, so significant that they will outlast all other great quotes.
Has the greatest quote of all changed your life?

If you do what you've always done....

Outline

How do we live for God? What does that mean? What do we need to do for us to truly "live for God"?

Opening

If you do what you've always done, then you will get what you've always got!

I remember hearing this phrase and realising it was true of all areas of life. It's used in business as a way of challenging people to do things differently. It is true of hobbies or sport that unless you change what you do, then you won't get any better. Don't expect to be a better footballer, golfer and runner unless you practise and improve or change what you currently do.

It's obvious when you think about it; in everything that we have learnt throughout our childhood and teenage years, we have had to change and improve what we do in order to "get better". When you were a baby you sat and cried when you wanted something, then you learnt that by pointing and making noises people would bring you the thing you wanted. The next stage was when you found out you could move, slowly, on your tummy and you shuffled to the object you wanted. Then as you grew stronger you crawled and scrambled across the room. Next you could stand and move around furniture. Eventually the first steps and walking became a reality. Freedom and chaos ensued! Finally came running and the ability to get where you wanted to be at speed (well for some of us at speed, for others slightly quicker than crawling!)

So we learn to change how we move as we develop in order to find the fastest and best way to get where we want to be. (For some this then evolves to driving and your parents then recall the easier days when you sat and pointed!)

So what of this issue then of how we live for God? How do we do it?

The reality is that living for God involves becoming more like Jesus Christ. Becoming more like Jesus means that you can't stay as you are now. The parts of you that are not like Him or if we are honest – totally unlike Him – need to change.

The apostle Paul wrestles with this thought when he says *"I do not understand what I do. For what I want to do I do not do, but what I hate I do"* (Romans 7:15.)

So even one of the most faithful, influential, fearless Christians that ever lived says that he struggles not to do what he has always done.

The gospel writer John speaking of Jesus says, *"He must become greater; I must become less."* (John 3:30)

So we know what we need to do, but how do we do it? When was the last time that you seriously looked at your life and identified the things that need to change? Are you in that comfort zone of "I am not that bad, I am doing ok and those things that make me happy aren't really hurting anyone."

So today let's be ruthless! What areas of your life stop you developing or stop you growing as a Christian? What areas are totally unlike Jesus? Okay let's be clear about what kinds of things we should give up but may not want to; WHAT WE WATCH ON TV, WHAT WE READ, SWEARING, DRINKING, SEXUAL BEHAVIOUR, FRIENDS THAT ENCOURAGE ANY OF THIS, TEMPER, FIGHTING, CAUSING PROBLEMS WITH OTHER PEOPLE BY BACK STABBING AND SAYING WHAT WE SHOULDN'T...... THE LIST IS ENDLESS.

Teach

Do you really want to grow? Do you really want to live for God? Are you happy living a life with a foot in both camps? If you are serious then pray about the things on this list that need to change, ask God to help you change these things. Don't be embarrassed, He already knows what you have said and done! He loves you still and He wants you to change, He wants you to soar, to have a faith and a joy that comes from living for Him.

> *He wants you to soar, to have a faith and a joy that comes from living for Him.*

BUT just like crawling to walking to running, it doesn't happen overnight and there are bumps on the way! It takes time and effort on your part. Being more like Jesus involves spending more time with Him. It means having an honesty about your prayers that wasn't there before. It means honestly assessing what needs to go and choosing not to do those things anymore. You may fail, you may fall down. Pray and God will pick you back up again, just like the parent encouraging the young toddler to walk. Spend time reading your Bible. Spend time with Christian friends who will encourage and challenge you.

Choose not to do what you have always done.

However this rule can also be a positive thing; continue to do the things in your life that encourage your faith. Think about the things that produce love, peace, patience, kindness and do these often!

Reach

Maybe you think we are talking nonsense, why give up what you enjoy? If it makes you happy, go for it! If that ethos is true then why are so many people who pursue all the things above and more, so miserable? Does everything you do bring you joy and a feeling of contentment?

> *God doesn't expect you to do it all on your own*

Jesus said *"I have come that they may have life, and have it to the full"* (John 10:10).

If you do what you have always done (lived without Jesus) then you will get what you have always got (a life that is less full than it could and should be).

God doesn't expect you to do it all on your own, He says let me help you change. By His Spirit He has changed people who the world had given up on. So today He asks...do you want to keep doing what you always have done or do you want life to the full?

Conflict!

Outline

What should we do when we come into conflict with one another? Does the Bible teach us anything about if or how we should deal with arguments?

Opening

Isn't life great when you can have time with your friends doing things that you enjoy? The days where you have spent the day together, maybe a summers day at the park or the beach or playing football and then a barbeque at night. Days and nights that you talk about for weeks, months, years to come and still laugh and smile about what was said and done. Great days when you shared time with people that you care about and shared common interests and enjoyment. Days like that don't happen often enough, do they?

In the Bible it says that *"whatever is noble, whatever is right, whatever is pure, whatever is lovely, whatever is admirable, think about such things"* (Philippians 4:8)

It's good to think about good things! So why then do we often get preoccupied with the people and the things that make life difficult or disappointing? Sadly we all have people that we encounter at times who make life uncomfortable and we come into conflict with them. It is also worth remembering that whilst you may have a picture of someone in your head who makes you angry or unhappy – that right now – you may be the person in someone else's mind! So as we look at this subject we need to always be examining our own behaviour first!

So what do you do with this person or people who infuriate you? What are the possible actions that you can take?

- Fight – physical or verbal
- Flee – walk away and avoid them
- Fuel the fire – try to gain support for your view by canvassing others and talking about them
- Friendship – try and build bridges and overcome the issues

Maybe you're thinking, "that's easy for you to say, you don't know what this person has said or done to me". We are all human and whether we show it or not we are hurt by people who say things about us or whose actions hurt us by excluding us or belittling us or betraying us.

It's very important to say that we are talking here about arguments and conflict that are "normal". Anything that relates to bullying or abuse of any kind must be dealt with and it's very important that you speak to someone you trust, who can help you.

 Teach

What did Jesus do with people who treated Him badly? Well brace yourself because this is a tough act to follow! How many verses can I quote you?

1. Turn the other cheek (Matthew 5:39)
2. Forgive your brother seventy seven times (Matthew 18:22)
3. Forgive as you have been forgiven (Colossians 3:13)
4. Pray for those who ill treat you (Luke 6:28)
5. Even as they crucified Him, Jesus says *"Father forgive them for they do not know not what they are doing"* (Luke 23:34)

But, and there is a "but", Jesus stood His ground when confronted with people who challenged His authority and His views on the world. We are not called to be doormats that people walk all over or to be forced to do things that we don't want to do. Jesus also turned over the tables of money changers in the temple in righteous anger (please please don't turn the kitchen table over next time there is a family dispute over dinner – that's not righteous anger) but again this shows that at times it is right that we should be angry. The difficulty is how and when we show that emotion.

> We are not called to be doormats...

Jesus demonstrated a balance of meekness and strength that has never been seen before or since. I believe that is our guide. We should aim to be a person who does not intimidate or bully others but rather a person who has strength and a confidence that comes from our faith in Jesus Christ.

There is a very important verse in Matthew Chapter 5 that says that if we come to worship God and harbour ill feeling towards someone else, then we should examine ourselves. The verse says that if you know you have a grudge then *"leave your gift there in front of the altar. First go and be reconciled to your brother; then come and offer your gift"* (Matthew 5:23).

Verses like this aren't in the Bible to be read and ignored; God is serious that He wants you and me to worship Him with hearts that are right. Will we always agree as Christians? No. Should we always make sure that ill feeling and hurts are dealt with and forgiven? Yes. This means that where we are at fault we need to ask the forgiveness of others.

> *He wants you and me to worship Him with hearts that are right.*

 Reach

Is forgiveness a complete mystery to you? Do you have the mindset that once someone crosses you then that's it forever, "their card is marked"? Maybe you sort things out by giving as good as you get, maybe you sort things out with words or even fists? (This can be true of anyone regardless of whether they are a Christian or not!)

Romans Chapter 5 verse 10 says once you were "God's enemies". Enemies? Do you have enemies? People that you really don't like, people you would rather avoid, maybe you would even say that you "hate" them! That verse goes on to say that it was while we were enemies of God that Jesus died for us.

So you and I were opposed to all that God wanted for us, ignoring Him, living for ourselves, enemies of God and what does He do? Strike us down, wipe us all out, start again, squash us?

No, He sends His Son to die for us; to say I love you, I extend my hand of friendship to you, I will make the first move despite the fact that you are in the wrong. It makes you think, doesn't it? Will you accept His hand of friendship safe in the knowledge that God will forgive?

Will you accept His hand of friendship...?

What are you worth?

Outline

We live in a world fixated by money and fame, where people are valued depending on who they are, what they do and how much they have. So based on that, what are we worth? More importantly what are we worth to God?

Opening

What do you think you are worth? How do you judge what others are worth?

Here are some figures: *(you may want to use other names or figures)*

- In 1902 the British football transfer record was £520 for Alf Common who moved from Sheffield Utd to Sunderland.
- In 2011 the record was set at £50 million for Fernando Torres when he joined Chelsea from Liverpool. Is he worth £50 million? What do we mean by "is he worth it?"
- Tiger Woods agreed a deal with Nike worth £90 million to wear clothes and use their clubs! Buick paid him £25 million to have Buick written on his golf bag!
- Frank Lampard is paid £140,000 a week to play football (that's £7.28 million a year)
- Bill Gates topped the world's rich list at $56 billion (or approx £31 billion) But this figure grows all the time.

There is a list each year of the most powerful people in sport/entertainment called the top 100. People are ranked on earnings and also "attributes" such as attractiveness, sex appeal, talent and intelligence. Tom Cruise has topped the poll with a meagre $67 million but scored high on attractiveness and talent. In 2011 Oprah was quoted in the Forbes rich list with $2.7 billion but Mark Zuckerberg of Facebook fame is worth $13.5 billion. Are we worth more if we are attractive or talented or rich?

You are worth different things to different people. If someone doesn't know you they may say "they don't mean anything to me" but to your friends and family you are highly valued.

Teach

What about your worth to God? He created you and therefore He knows your true value. When a designer makes a dress or Ferrari make a car they decide how much it is worth based on all the work that has gone into the dress or the car. Of all the things that God created including planets, solar systems, animals and mountains, it is you and I that He has valued above all other things. It is you and I that have been made in God's own image. We could not be more valuable to God than we are!

Philippians 3:7-8 *"I once thought these things were valuable, but now I consider them worthless because of what Christ has done. Yes, everything else is worthless when compared with the infinite value of knowing Christ Jesus my Lord. For His sake I have discarded everything else, counting it all as garbage, so that I could gain Christ."*

This was how highly Paul valued Jesus. Paul had realised how valuable he was to God and how much God had done for him. He had discovered that God's Son, the promised Messiah had died for him.

> *We could not be more valuable to God than we are!*

The question is, have **you** counted everything else as garbage? Is Jesus still worth more than anything else in your life? When you became a Christian, you acknowledged that your priorities were wrong and asked God to change that. Your value to God is that you are worth the life of His Son. So how do you value Jesus? Do you value Him as much as having the right things? Do you squeeze Him in amongst all the things you know are wrong or squeeze a prayer in every other day? He is worth more than that; in fact He is beyond value.

 Reach

God created you. Sadly He knew that you would wander away and be far from Him during your life. He decided to buy you back. From whom you may ask? We were lost, separated from God and until our sin was forgiven we would be unable to be with God. God is perfect and Heaven is perfect so no sin can exist in Heaven but you and I sin almost from birth…. Everyone does!

Galatians 2:20 *"I have been crucified with Christ and I no longer live, but Christ lives in me. The life I live in the body, I live by faith in the Son of God, who loved me and gave himself for me."*

God devised a plan; He would buy you back by transferring all your sins from you and onto His Son Jesus. When Jesus died on the cross He had accepted all of your sins, they had been transferred to Him. He took your sin and suffered the pain of separation from His Father. But just like in football, there is a transfer deadline, a date when all transfers have to be completed or they can't happen. So God has put a transfer offer on the table to you; it says that He will forgive all your sins, that He will be with you forever and take you to Heaven when you die and be your strength each day. But in return you have to turn from the sins that caused your separation from God and live for Him. The offer is on the table, will you accept it?

> God has put a transfer offer on the table to you

When is the transfer deadline? Only God knows; it could be today or it could be 100 years. All we know is that when we die or when Jesus returns (one day Jesus will return to take Christians with Him to Heaven) the deadline closes and no more transfers can be completed. The moment we die or Jesus returns will be the time that closes the transfer window. For those people that have not become Christians, it will then be too late.

What are you worth?.... The life of the Son of God who loves you and gave himself for you.

What is He worth to you?....

KISS : Keep it simple stupid

Outline

Why do we find it so hard to talk about our faith and is it possible to do it simply and effectively? Encourage all the Christians tonight to KISS when sharing their faith: Keep it Simple Stupid.

Opening

Two young girls are out in the street playing, they are young (5&6) and one of them is a Christian. She is excited because she has invited her friend to Sunday School and her friend has accepted. She had been invited before but this time the answer is yes. The conversation then goes something like this,

> "If you come to Sunday school we will be like twins"
> "Yes 'cos then I will be a Christian too"
> "Well you're not a Christian if you just go to Sunday school, you have to ask Jesus into your heart"
> "How do I do that?"
> "You have to say a prayer"
> "What prayer?"
> "The prayer you say when you become a Christian, when you tell Jesus that you are sorry for all the wrong things that you have done and that you love Him and want Him to come into your heart"
> "I won't remember all of that"
> "That's ok, I will say it and you can just say it after me"

And so they did!

Where did this happen? On the pavement outside the friend's house whilst both stood on their scooters!

Straight after this, the girls continued playing and were on the trampoline where the girl was heard to say "now that you are a Christian, we can read my Bible together" and the friend replied "why don't you go and get it then." When she was asked about her friend being a Christian the girl replied "I'm a Christian now" and the girl added "Yes 'cos she's got Jesus in her heart."

Teach

What do we struggle with most as Christians? Probably telling others about our faith and if we do, then trying to make it sound slightly less complicated than nuclear physics!

The 6 year old girl in the story has no fear about her faith, no embarrassment; she just wants her friend to have what she has. So there is no hesitation to invite a friend to church and then no problems explaining in simple terms what she believes.

What a lesson to us all!

> My job is not to know these things but to **simply** trust in the God who knows all things.

Do I know exactly how the engine, fuel injection and automatic gearbox in my car work? I don't have a clue, but I know that if I push the accelerator, I go and if I push the brake, I stop. Do I know why God loves me and why there is suffering and when the world will end? No! But I believe in a God who knows all these things and more. My job is not to know these things but to **simply** trust in the God who knows all things.

Her faith is simple; she loves Jesus, He loves her. He died for her and she has asked Him to be in her heart. We can all share that message, can't we?

Think of someone that you can share your faith with this week. Think of someone that you would love to see becoming a Christian and pray that God would give you the chance to have a simple conversation with them.

✝ Reach

Jesus spoke about faith like this; He said that you need to have a child like faith to enter Heaven. (Mark 10:15)

So, all you have to do is say a prayer and that's it? Yes and No. Jesus said that not everyone who simply cries Lord will be saved but does say that if you confess your sin and believe in your heart that Jesus is Lord, then you will be saved. (Matthew 7:21 and Romans 10:9)

So how can you state **simply** what a Christian is?.... A person who has asked God for forgiveness, acknowledged that Jesus is God's Son and asked Him to be in their life.

1 John 5:11-12 *"And this is the testimony: God has given us eternal life, and this life is in His Son. He who has the Son has life; he who does not have the Son of God does not have life."*

This life starts as soon as you become a Christian and lasts for eternity.

When you get to Heaven there will not be the equivalent of your Physics Standard Grade/GCSE in order to gain entry or a record of whether you scored highly enough on the "good person" chart. No, it will be simple; do you have God's Son? If you do, then you will have life. This life starts as soon as you become a Christian and lasts for eternity. It's a new kind of life where your hope, your joy and your direction are all found in your relationship with God.

34

What if...?

Outline

There are so many questions in life, so many unknowns but also a few certainties. As Christians we believe in the Bible, in order, a plan and a purpose. Does this stop us asking what if?

Opening

Someone once said that golf should have been called "If" because everyone that plays golf always says "if only I hadn't played that shot" or "if only I had holed that putt" or "if only I had thought about that"... If!

What would be the ifs in your life at the moment?

- If only you had studied last year.......
- If only that hadn't happened...
- If only you had the courage to ask him/her out....
- If only your mum and dad understood that you need.....
- If only your mum and dad would just leave you alone....
- If only you could look like him then you would be.......
- If you had this then you would be happy.......
- If only someone cared.........

Lots of these ifs can be translated as why can't you be like that or why can't you have that or why can't things be better. It is normal to ask these questions sometimes, often just to yourself when you feel down.

Life is full of ifs. It's full of uncertainty and lots and lots of things that we don't know, but we also think if only I knew...

- If only I knew what people thought of me...(then I would be happy/or change)
- If only I knew when I would die...(then I would know what to do and by when)
- If only I knew if there was really a God...

What about certainties? Are there any?

- Just as you were born, one day you will die
- You were created by God (via your mum and dad!)
- You are loved by God
- One day you will meet God
- Jesus died on the cross for you

Whether you believe these things and trust in them is key to your eternity.

Teach

Do you spend enough time thinking about the certainties in life?

You are loved by God… You are forgiven… You will spend forever in Heaven when you die… When you pray God hears and answers your prayers… God wants the very best for you

Jeremiah 29:11 *"For I know the plans I have for you, declares the Lord, plans to prosper you and not to harm you, plans to give you hope and a future."*

Okay Christian here are a couple of other what ifs for you:

> **What would happen if you really committed yourself to living for God?**

What would happen if you really committed yourself to living for God? What are you missing out on if you don't live for God? What happens if you don't talk to your friends about your faith? If you knew that you couldn't fail, what would you do for God?

You could be living life in God's strength; doing things that you never imagined you could do. You could be seeing your friends becoming Christians and together you could be serving God. Think about what this would do for your faith, your friendships and your church.

Let's not get to Heaven and think "if only".

Reach

What are you thinking? What if you believe in this and it's not true? What if you give up stuff and miss out on stuff and it's all for nothing. It won't be, but let me ask you this…what if it's true (and it is) and you don't believe it? How much more do you have to lose?

God has sent His Son into the world for you. Now He waits for the world to respond. Do you think that if you respond to Him that He will remain silent? No. When you become a Christian God gives you that certainty, that peace that can only come from Him.

2 Chronicles 7:14 *"**If** my people, who are called by my name, will humble themselves and pray and seek my face and turn from their wicked ways, then will I hear from heaven and will forgive their sin."*
It's a big "if"; so much depends on you believing. If you humble yourself and pray then God will hear from Heaven and forgive, **but** only if you humbly seek God and ask Him to help you change.

so much depends on you believing

If only you would believe that this is true.

If only you will take a step of faith and realise for yourself that it's true.

The real thing?

Outline

Are young people living a life that is aimed at fitting in, saying and doing all the things that make sure they fit in? Is that what we are called to do?

Preparation

Take with you 3 cans of coke, 2 of which should be full and 1 empty (make a small hole in the bottom so that the ring pull is not different to the other two). Place them on a table for the group to see but not touch.

Ask 3 volunteers to pick a can each which they can all keep. All 3 look the same and could be empty but only 1 is not the "real thing".

Opening

Being a teenager is probably the hardest decade of a person's life! Here are just some of the pressures that come during this period,

Puberty
Hormones
New school
New friends
Pressure to fit in with the crowd, to speak and act in a certain way
Pressure to wear the right labels from head to toe
Pressure from parents
Fighting with parents (do teenagers do this?)
Exams
Homework (do teenagers do this?
First girlfriend/boyfriend
Peer pressure with sex/drink/drugs
The right results for university or college
Finding a job
Trying to be who you want to be versus who others think you should be
Trying to be who God made you to be

So what do most teenagers do? They go through secondary school wearing the mask that says am I bothered? who cares? And I am confident being me. The trouble is we all do this on the outside but only God really sees the inside. He knows what we truly think, what we feel and who we are when no-one else is around.

1 Samuel 16:7 *"The Lord does not look at the things that man looks at. Man looks at the outward appearance, but the Lord looks at the heart."* You can kid your mum and dad or your pals, but you can never kid God. He knows exactly what you feel and think, He made you and no-one understands you as well as God does.

What would you change about your life if you thought that it would not harm your friendships? What would you do if it made no difference to what people think of you?

God says that everyone looks at the outward appearance, what people wear, whether they are confident, good looking, drive a good car, live in a big house or buy designer clothes.

But God looks past all that into our hearts and knows everything that we desire (good or bad). He knows every thought we have. It would be like having x-ray vision with the coke cans and seeing which one was empty on the inside. Don't spend your life living to please everyone else, you will never do it! It's impossible to please friends, family, teachers and yourself.

Teach

Would I know by watching you that you are a Christian? If I followed you for a day would you look the same and do the same things as everyone else? Could I tell if you were empty or full? We are called to be different, to be filled with the "real thing". The Pepsi challenge was an advert a while ago for Pepsi where people had to try two different types of cola and they were certain that they would be able to tell the difference – that Pepsi was better! Your friends will be watching your life and the lives of other friends, do they see a difference? Would you pass the Pepsi challenge? The difference is that the people didn't know what was on the inside until they had a drink (the coke was in plain cups) but as Christians our lives should show that what we have inside is different. We have Christ in our hearts and that must make a difference to the way that we live. People need to hear and see that Jesus makes a difference in our lives.

> *our lives should show that what we have inside is different*

Galatians 5:22 *"But the fruit of the Spirit is love, joy, peace, patience, kindness, goodness, faithfulness, gentleness and self-control..."* How many of them have you demonstrated over the past week?

Reach

Who do you live to please? Yourself? Really? Then why is what you wear, what you listen to and what you watch the same as your friends? What is your life filled with? Is it all just a front, like the empty can? Is coke just coke, they all taste the same? No. Are we all the same, just humans who live, die and that's it? No. The Bible says you are made for a purpose and that every individual is made for a specific reason. You are not just a can of coke that is the same as billions of other cans of coke, you are unique. Do you want to know why God created you and what plans He has for you?

Jeremiah 29:11 *"For I know the plans I have for you, declares the Lord, plans to prosper you and not to harm you, plans to give you hope and a future..."*

Jesus said that He came so that you may have life and live life to the full (John 10:10). So what is your life full of? Coca Cola's slogan was the real thing, meaning others may copy us but we are the original and the best. Jesus offers you life, the best life and real life. The choice is yours, both look the same but only one is full of the real thing.

Psalm 34:8 *"Taste and see that the Lord is good"*

Pepsi's advert, the "Pepsi challenge" challenged people to taste their product versus another coke. They believed that once you had tasted both, you would choose Pepsi as the better cola. *"Taste and see that the Lord is good"*; He is offering you the real thing.

Are you listening?

Outline

God speaks to us all, but do we hear Him? Do we want to hear Him? It is important that we listen to God because one day His voice on Earth will no longer be heard. If we hear His voice, we need to respond.

Preparation

Possibly incorporate a brief music quiz – how good are they at recognising voices? Play 10 introductions to current or well known songs and ask them to guess who is singing. Or if you are brave, record the leaders singing or saying something funny.

Opening

> What do you listen to? *Choose a couple of people in the group who you have already asked and talk about their taste in music.* Is it a boyband or X Factor winners? Do you listen to music because you enjoy it or it gives your feelings a voice or is it cool to be listening to rap regardless of whether you like it or not?
>
> What about with your friends; do you like to listen to gossip, or to people slagging others off? Do you worry what is being said when you are not there? Are they talking about me? What about those voices inside, sometimes pulling in opposite directions? It's very tough; you spend 30 hours a week in school with friends who do and say things that you are part of and just accept and then you have this voice inside that says "this isn't right". What can happen is that we convince ourselves that a little compromise is okay, they're my friends, it won't hurt, I will be "Norman no mates" if I don't do it! But God loves you and wants the best for you, His desire is that you believe and trust in HIM.

Teach

Psalm 95:7-10 *"We are the people He watches over, the sheep under His care. Oh, that you would listen to His voice today. The Lord says, Don't harden your hearts as Israel did at Meribah. For there your ancestors tried my patience; they courted my wrath though they had seen many miracles."*(The Living Bible)

You have already experienced the Lord's blessing, seen Him work in your life, so why have you stopped listening? Can you remember what it was like when you first became a Christian, everything seemed so clear, so certain, you were going to follow Jesus and listen to Him.

Can you think of a time when you were sure that God was speaking to you? *(You may want to tell about a time when God has spoken to you.)*

God has spoken to you in the past and wants to speak to you every day. What is He telling you to do?

God speaks through your daily reading of the Bible or Bible notes and when you pray to Him. That's why it is so important to have daily reading notes and read your Bible each day. For some people this time may involve walking, praying and being somewhere quiet with God. He will speak to you through youth groups, teaching times at church and sometimes through Christian friends. Sometimes people will think you are mad as a Christian when you say you listen to God as if you have secret earphones for a magic iPod tucked away somewhere listening to God. But when you read the Bible or notes that really speak to you and think that's me – then that's God speaking to you!

If you can't hear the Lord's voice it's because you're not listening to Him

God sometimes asks you to do things and other times it is a commandment or promise for you. Are you baptised? The Bible is clear that God commands all Christians to be baptised as a witness to those around us that you have trusted in Him and died to your old life.

Is He speaking to you? Are you ignoring Him? If you can't hear the Lord's voice it's because you're not listening to Him; you are too far away and you need to get closer to Him. How do I do that? Get back to spending time with Him, reading your Bible and praying each day. God won't be quiet when you come to Him asking for Him to speak to you.

 Reach

Revelation 3:20 *"Look! Here I stand at the door and knock. If you hear me calling and open the door, I will come in."*

God speaks to you too!

But not as a guide and not to encourage. God says simply, I love you and I want you to trust in me. God wants to bless you, direct you and speak to you but He needs your attention first. The Bible has one strong message from beginning to end; God loves you.

God created the universe, the heavens, the Earth and all that are in them. Everything speaks of God as the creator. God created you as an individual and then sent His Son to Earth to make amends for all of your mistakes that were keeping you far from Him. This tells you that God is a loving Father who wants to help you and protect you.

He stands in front of you today and says I want to come in.

He stands in front of you today and says I want to come in. If I came to your house and knocked at your door but there was no answer, how long would I wait? How many times would I knock or ring the bell before I gave up?

God says to you today, here I am for you! I hope you are listening because He is speaking to YOU!

Heaven, we have a problem!

Outline

To look at our purpose in life; why are we here and what were we made to do? We have all been made for a purpose.

Resources

Apollo 13 – show the clip of the astronauts looking out at the moon as it passes by (scene 6 on the DVD)

![opening icon] Opening

> Apollo 13 is a great film. It tells the real life story of American astronauts trying to land on the moon. Shortly after launch there is an explosion and very quickly the astronauts know that they will not be able to land on the moon. In that one second the mission changes, it's no longer about landing on the moon, it's about survival and will they make it home?
>
> None of the astronauts had ever been to the moon. For Fred Haise (one of the astronauts) it would be his last time in space. Fred had trained his whole life for this event; studying, training as a pilot, working with NASA and whatever else you need to do to be an astronaut! Everything was working towards the goal of landing on the moon. It never happened. Apollo 13 circled the moon and the astronauts got agonisingly close, but never actually set foot on the moon.
>
> So what is your life preparing you for? What is your mission in life? God has given you gifts and abilities that He wants you to use for Him. They can be things you are good at, things you enjoy, sport, music, being friendly etc. Are you using the gifts you have been given? Can you imagine an astronaut training for years and then getting the chance to go on the spaceship but saying "no thanks I am happy playing about on a computer game!"

![cross icon] Reach

You can come to church, come to youth group, read your Bible, pray but it doesn't make you a Christian. You can be close, but just like Apollo 13 it's like being a million miles away from the moon. To be a Christian is like landing on the moon, you know you are there. Your vision changes; rather than looking up at the moon you are looking back at the Earth, where you used to be. To be a Christian is to know God's forgiveness and His peace. Fred Haise has the sadness of a man who never fulfilled his purpose; he was close but never actually got there. Don't be nearly a Christian...make sure! Jesus once met a rich young ruler who asked how he could get to Heaven. Jesus told him about the commandments and then challenged him about the importance the man placed on money – in other words Jesus is saying, I must be the most important thing in your life. Mark 10:22 says *"At this the man's face fell. He went away sad, because he had great wealth."*

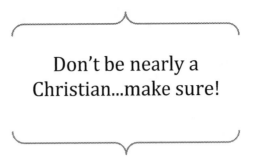

Don't be nearly a Christian...make sure!

There is no middle ground, you are either opting in or opting out!

To be on the moon must be amazing, to feel the dust under your boots and look down at the planet Earth and know that very few people have ever done what you are doing. To be nearly on the moon, or just look at the moon is not quite the same. To look at someone who is a Christian and think "nah that's not for me" or say "I believe God exists but I don't want to do anything about it" is like just looking at the moon. The shuttle is here and the doors are open. Do you want to experience the moon for yourself? Christians are people who have experienced God's forgiveness and love for themselves. Are you ready for a new mission in life?

 Teach

What is your purpose? You were made to serve God and you were made to please God.

I wonder if I asked everyone in your class at school, who is a Christian in this class or in this school, would they choose you? Are you different? Do they see you with a mission? A purpose to life?

Ephesians 5:8 *"For you were once darkness, but now you are light in the Lord. Live as children of light"* God has called you as a witness for Him; to witness to those you go to school with, play football with, your family and friends. Have you fallen back into your old ways, has the mission got tough? God doesn't do failed missions! Keep focused on your mission.

Becoming a Christian should change you forever.

Are you living out your purpose for God or like Fred Haise are you watching it pass you by?

If I took you to the moon, you would talk about it every day. You would never be the same. It would change your view of life. Becoming a Christian should change you forever. You should want to talk about it all the time.

Have you achieved what God has given you to do? Have you even got out of the spaceship? When the astronauts walked on the moon they left footprints in the dust. Whether you realise it or not others are following in your footprints. As you live out your mission for God on earth, show others the way and let them see what an adventure it is to be a Christian.

As others see your footprints may you live with the joy and purpose of someone who has experienced something better than landing on the moon.

God created evil: true or false?

 Outline

To look at the reality of a life without God or the danger for Christians in not spending time with God.

Opening

Have you ever been told a story that turned out to be an urban myth? One myth surrounds a story about Einstein and it is a good story.

An atheist professor asks his class "Did God create everything?"
"Yes" replies a brave student.
"Then God created evil as evil exists and as we are what we create then God must be evil" stated the Prof. The brave student shrinks in his seat.

Then another student (Einstein) speaks from the back of the room, "Can I ask a question?... Professor, does cold exist?"
"Of course it does," laughs the Prof, "have you never been cold" he scoffs.
The young man replied "Actually it doesn't, according to the laws of physics cold is simply the absence of heat, heat is what makes a body or matter have energy. Absolute zero (-460F) is the total absence of heat where all matter becomes inert. Cold does not exist; it is simply a word to describe the absence of heat."

The young man continued "Professor, does darkness exist?"
The Prof now a bit less cocky says "Of course it does."
The student replies "Again you are wrong, darkness does not exist, darkness is the absence of light. We can measure light but how do you measure darkness? Simply by the absence of light! Darkness is a word used to describe the absence of light."

Finally the student asks "Professor, does Evil exist?"
The Prof replies indignantly "Of course it does, every day we read about or hear of murder, theft and the like. Evil exists!"

The student replied "Evil does not exist, at least not on its own. Evil is the absence of God. Just like darkness or cold, a word man has invented to describe the absence of something. God did not create evil. God created love and faith just like heat and light. Evil is what happens when a man does not have God's love in his heart, like cold where there is no heat or darkness where there is no light."

The Professor sat down.

Teach

- Are you struggling to grow in your faith?
- Are you struggling to tell your friends what you believe?
- Are you struggling to be interested in youth group or church?
- Are you struggling to pray?
- Is your language or behaviour becoming a problem?

The biggest myth you can believe as a Christian is that you can survive without spending time with God each day. No quiet time leads to an absence of God, which leads to problems. Where God is absent it will be filled by other things. You will fill your time and your life with things that often are not pleasing to God. It could be things that you watch on television, music that you listen to or things you do with friends.

Make sure you have daily notes that work for you and use them. If you want to grow, want to witness, want God's presence – read and pray daily. If you have a friend that moves house and you don't see them for some time then they will have changed and so will you. You have lost touch and maybe when you meet up you don't have as much in common as you had before.

Spending time with God is not just once a day for five minutes but it is having a continuous awareness of God throughout the day. Do you pray to God throughout the day for help or to say thank you? When you lose touch with God you deviate from the way that He would want you to live.

> *When you lose touch with God you deviate from the way that He would want you to live.*

Matthew 4:4 *"It is written; Man does not live on bread alone, but on every word that comes from the mouth of God."* Jesus is very clear about this that if Christians don't read their Bible and listen to God they won't be healthy just as you can't possibly be healthy if you don't eat the right food. Have you been starving yourself or eating too much junk food?

When you don't spend time with God you allow the devil to get a foothold in your life.

Reach

"Absence of God is Evil"

God looks at Christians and sees Jesus in them (they are far from perfect but God sees Jesus in them). God looks at non-Christians and loves them but sees sin because they do not have Jesus in their lives. When a Christian has met with God they know that Jesus is no myth and they are forgiven for their sin. What will you do when you realise what you thought was a myth is actually true? Will it be too late? A myth is simply a made up story. Jesus died on a wooden cross, and lay in a stone tomb but He came back to life two days later and has changed the lives of

> If you believe the life of Jesus is a myth there are millions of people who would argue that their life proves it isn't.

millions of people who have trusted in Him. This is not a myth, it's a reality! Two thousand years on our calendar is set by His birth. If you believe the life of Jesus is a myth there are millions of people who would argue that their life proves it isn't.

2 Corinthians 5:20 *"We are therefore Christ's ambassadors, as though God were making His appeal through us. We implore you on Christ's behalf: Be reconciled to God. God made him who had no sin to be sin for us, so that in Him we might become the righteousness of God."*

One day you will know that for sure that God wanted you to be reconciled to Him, please make sure you can look forward to that day. Be reconciled today and live in the good of God's presence.

When was Noel Edmonds cool?

Outline

To look at what we gain through faith in Jesus Christ and what we might think we have to lose.

Opening

Everyone now knows Noel Edmonds for "Deal or no Deal" but once upon a time he was the king of Saturday morning children's TV in a programme called "Swap Shop". The best bit of the programme was when people who wanted to swap toys they didn't want anymore like a BMX bike phoned in.. They would ask to swap the BMX for a computer game or anything else they wanted. It was great and it always surprised me what people would swap things for! Like Nigel in Norfolk wanting to swap a cricket bat for a goldfish. We still swap things today, isn't it weird that we swap a bit of paper for things but trust that the bit of paper (money) is worth something. We hand over a ten pound note and get given a CD! We work in a shop or delivering papers and someone gives us a bit of paper for all our efforts but we trust that it is worth something.

So what is the best swap ever done?

Isaiah 53:5 *"But He was pierced for our transgressions….. the punishment that brought us peace was upon Him and by His wounds we are healed."*

2 Corinthians 5:21 *"God made Him who had no sin to be sin for us, so that in Him we might become the righteousness of God."*

Jesus swapped His home in Heaven for a life on Earth, but even better for us, He swapped perfection for our sins, He swapped life in Heaven for a life on Earth and death on a wooden cross. That doesn't seem much of a swap does it? However the reason Jesus swapped Heaven for Earth was so that you could swap Earth for Heaven!

Reach

What will you swap? The Bible says that sin causes you to look dirty to God, in other words your sins can be seen by God and look like you are wearing filthy rags (even if you think your jeans are the best there is) God says that there is no sin in Heaven and He cannot allow filthy rags in Heaven. So what do you do? Jesus makes you this offer – I will swap my perfect white clothes for your filthy rags – in other words I will take all your sin and swap you for complete forgiveness. God's peace, spiritual resources that are beyond your imagination, Gods will in your life and of course the small matter of eternal life (which is kind of like an all-inclusive holiday in the best place you can ever imagine, with the best of everything and more!!). Sounds like a good deal! What do you need to do? Trust in Him. Is that it? Yes. You will want to swap when you realise that you have nothing of any real value to swap God with but He is willing to give you it all if you simply acknowledge that you need what He is offering.

Imagine Christmas Eve and you have no money, but would love to have lots of great things but you know it's not possible. God's swap is the equivalent of you throwing all the worst rubbish you have in your bin and in the morning it has been replaced with the best stuff and better than you ever asked for. You would jump at a swap like that but God's swap is better than that!

[*He offers you the best deal of your life*] Jesus loves you and died for you, He offers you the best deal of your life. Your sin for His forgiveness. A life of sin for eternal life. Is your life now so good that it is worth more than the life that Jesus offers you?

2 Corinthians 5:15 *"And He died for all, that those who live should no longer live for themselves but for Him who died for them and was raised again."* The deal isn't that you take God's gift of life and then carry on as before, living life your way. Rather you should change and want to live to please God because you acknowledge all that He has done for you.

Like all good deals it only lasts for a limited time, that is until Jesus returns or you die (whichever comes first). In the meantime, think about what you are missing out on and not what you may have to give up!

 Teach

What are you wearing? Isaiah 61:10 says *"I am overwhelmed with joy in the LORD my God! For He has dressed me with the clothing of salvation and draped me in a robe of righteousness. I am like a bridegroom in his wedding suit or a bride with her jewels."* Do you live like you are still wearing those filthy rags or do you live like you are wearing clothes that cost more than anything you can ever buy? The clothes you have are the most expensive that have ever been made, they cost God's Son His life! As part of the swap when you became a Christian, the Holy Spirit began to live in you.

• • •

The clothes you have are the most expensive that have ever been made, they cost God's Son His life!

• • •

Would you wear brand new designer clothes to go swamp walking? No. Then think about what you say and do with God's Holy Spirit in you everyday. You carry God with you each day in your heart. The challenge is to live in such a way that those new clothes look better than anything you've ever worn. If you got the best deal or best swap you would use up all your credit on your mobile while you told your friends about it, why then are we so slow to talk about all we have been given as Christians?

- **Show the world that you wouldn't swap being a Christian for anything.**
- **Live in a way that those around want to know where you got those clothes.**

It's Unbelievable!

Outline

To examine the thought that some young people don't see the Christian message as believable, they may be taught it is a myth or a story. This talk is aimed at challenging their view of what they believe and why.

Opening

When I was young I used to play golf in the local school grounds opposite my house. One day I went up to play and accidentally hit a ball towards the house that was directly opposite mine! I just remember seeing the ball flying towards the windows at the back of the house and I ran all the way home! After tea I went for a bath and whilst in the bath the lady from that house across the road came to the door. I lay in the bath, panicking and thinking of what would happen when I got out and had to explain a broken window.

Sure enough when I got out of the bath, there was my mum with a golf ball in her hand, my golf ball. She told me the lady across the road had handed it in. I was just about to offer my excuses and apologies when my mum added that the lady was ironing her husband's clothes after taking them off the washing line and she found the ball in a pair of his pants! She knew I played golf and thought I might like the ball.

Now that's unbelievable! But it is true! I know because it happened to me.

You may say that the Bible is just a book and God is a man made creation, that Christians are weak people who just need something to believe. How do you know it's true? What if it's not true and you waste your life?

What if it is? Christians know that it is because just like the golf ball story, it is a personal experience. Christians have personally known the difference that being a Christian has brought in terms of forgiveness, peace, guidance and knowing that prayers have been answered. Ah that's just coincidence you say.

God says He knows every hair on your head, knew your every thought before you were born and one day He will meet you. 1 John 3: 2 *"and we can't even imagine what we will be like when Christ returns. But we do know that when He comes we will be like Him, for we will see Him as He really is."*

Unbelievable?

 Teach

If you believe this message then why does it not impact more on your life? As Christians we believe that we are going to Heaven because we have trusted in Jesus. As a result, we believe that those who have not trusted in Jesus are not going to Heaven. Romans 6:23 *"For the wages of sin is death, but the gift of God is eternal life in Christ Jesus our Lord."*

Does this affect how you are with your friends? Matthew 5:14-16 *"You are the light of the world. A city on a hill cannot be hidden. Neither do people light a lamp and put it under a bowl. Instead they put it on its stand, and it gives light to everyone in the house. In the same way, let your light shine before men, that they may see your good deeds and praise your Father in heaven."* Is this true of you?

Are you believable as a Christian?

Do you purposely hide what you have or is it set out for everyone to see?

If there was a trial and they accused you of being a Christian, would there be enough evidence to convict you? 2 Corinthians 3:18 *"And we, who with unveiled faces all reflect the Lord's glory, are being transformed into His likeness with ever-increasing glory, which comes from the Lord, who is the Spirit."* Is this true of you?

Reach

Amazing but true facts:

- If you are an average sleeper you will roll over in bed 12 times tonight.
- Injured fingernails grow faster than uninjured ones.
- Lions are the only cats to live in packs.
- At old English weddings, guests threw shoes at the groom.
- English is the language with the most words, nearly 1 million.
- Goldfish have a memory span of 3 seconds. (Twice as long as most boys!)

Whether you believe in God's love for you now or not, it is important that you know it's true. What do you believe? That this world is all there is, that we are all slime that evolved from a big bang, that all good people go to Heaven? Hebrews 11:6 *"And without faith it is impossible to please God, because anyone who comes to Him must believe that He exists and that He rewards those who earnestly seek Him."* You must have faith to please God.

Christians believe in the Bible because historically it has been shown to be accurate and most importantly the promises made in it have been found to be true. One day you will see and know that it is true but the question is will you believe now or only when it is too late?

2 Corinthians 6:2 *"For He says, "In the time of my favour I heard you, and in the day of salvation I helped you." I tell you, now is the time of God's favour, now is the day of salvation"*

Have you seen the adverts? Unbelievable sale or Unbelievable prices. The offer stands now, today, but we are told that one day the offer will end. When will you choose to believe that God's love is amazing but true?

What is your nickname?

Outline

To look at the subject of nicknames and why they are given. The term Christian was originally a nickname meaning "one belonging to Christ". Do we belong to Christ?

Preparation

Look at the nicknames of the leaders and young people in your group and why they came about. Try to find the nicknames of leaders when they were at school and when they lost that nickname. Were they embarrassed by the nickname? What about famous nicknames? Posh, Fergie etc

Opening

What nicknames have you been given and why? My only nicknames have been "DT" (my initials) and "Disco", which was given to me by a friend after I "danced" through the defence and scored a goal at football. (*Explain your nickname if this is easier*)

One friend was called "Diesel" after he accidentally put petrol into a diesel van on the first night of a youth weekend away (they spent 2 hours in a petrol station waiting for the AA to come and drain the tank!) Another leader had the nickname of "Bun" as his name was Hutchinson which was shortened to Hutch in which a bunny lives and so this was shortened to bun. Nicknames can also be cruel. At school I had some friends called: Podge (slightly overweight) wee man (below average height) and Spud (he had a head like a potato).

Nicknames are generally given to you by your friends and mean something to you and them. What about the term Christian? Where did that come from? It was at Antioch the Bible says that followers of Jesus were first called Christ-ians, meaning ones belonging to Christ. We don't know if the term was meant to be a derisory term or one which described that these people belonged to Jesus. But clearly this group stood out and people could tell who the Christians were.

Teach

1 Peter 3:15 *"But in your hearts set apart Christ as Lord. Always be prepared to give an answer to everyone who asks you to give the reason for the hope that you have. But do this with gentleness and respect."*

Are you in danger of being called a Christian? Do people even know what you believe? Belonging to Jesus is a great thing, something that brings a lot of benefits; such as forgiveness, peace, love and eternity in Heaven. Why then are you so embarrassed to be known as a Christian? Matthew 10:32-33 *"Whoever acknowledges me before men, I will also acknowledge Him before my Father in Heaven. But whoever disowns me before men, I will disown him before my Father in Heaven."*

Jesus said that whoever rejects Him, rejects the one who sent Him (God the Father). (Luke 10:16) If you are a Christian, then it is wrong to deny your faith; to deny the one who died for you. What does belonging to Jesus mean? It means that you live to please

> *Belonging to Jesus means being proud of the fact that you are a Christian*

Him, and try to live as Jesus did. Belonging to Jesus means being proud of the fact that you are a Christian, it means wanting your friends to have all that you have. If you really value all that you have as a Christian then why wouldn't you want your friends to know what you believe and what you have?

Do your friends have a nickname for you? Do they know that in Antioch you would be called a Christian? In Antioch would they have known you were a Christian? One day when you stand in Heaven you will be so pleased and relieved to be a Christian, you will know what it means to belong to Jesus. Wouldn't it be sad at that moment if you looked back at your life on Earth and realised that you had spent it being ashamed of belonging to Jesus, Christ-ian? Are you failing to do the most important job that God has given you? Yes you! Mark 16:15-16 *"He said to them, "Go into all the world and preach the good news to all creation. Whoever believes and is baptized will be saved, but whoever does not believe will be condemned." "*

Christian, that's your job. Go and live out your faith. Live out the fact that you belong to Christ.

Reach

I am sure you have written your nickname on your school books, bag, fences etc. Why? You probably like your nickname and it means something to you but it is just a name. The name Christian is given to those who have asked Jesus into their hearts and lives and asked Him for forgiveness. This isn't just a name, it carries with it the assurance that the Christian will spend the whole of eternity in Heaven with God. You may be called Dazza, Gazza or Monkey Boy. However what matters more than any other name is the name of Jesus because whether or not you accept Him and adopt the name Christian will determine where you spend eternity and how you spend your time on earth. 1 John 5:11-12 *"And this is the testimony: God has given us eternal life, and this life is in His Son. He who has the Son has life; he who does not have the Son of God does not have life."*

> *This isn't just a name; it carries with it the assurance that the Christian will spend the whole of eternity in Heaven with God.*

I can walk into my company's offices because my name is on the list of people who belong to the company. There is a list in Heaven of people who belong to Jesus; they are the ones who will be allowed in. Are you on that list? You can belong to a golf club, a gang, a football team or a youth club but none of those membership cards or badges will be enough to get you into Heaven. None of those clubs allow you to talk to God every day and know that He is with you every moment of your life. Belong to clubs, play sports because they're great fun but more importantly…

…make sure that you belong to Jesus because there is nothing better or more important than this.

Dear God, do you like my singing?

Outline

How do we know when God is happy with us? As Christians, do we live to please God? What can we do to live to please God?

Opening

> My daughter says her prayers each night before she goes to bed and one night her mum overheard this prayer,
>
> *"Dear God, I just wanted to ask you something"*
>
> Pause
>
> *"Did you see me today and did you like my singing?"*
>
> Pause
>
> *"I think that's a yes"*
>
> Pause
>
> *"Well I know you can hear me but I can't hear you but I'm sure you liked it even though I can't hear you"*
>
> What faith! No wonder the Bible talks about God looking for us to a have a child like faith…just simple honesty with God. Matthew 18:3 *"And He said: "I tell you the truth, unless you change and become like little children, you will never enter the kingdom of heaven." "*
>
> I love this story as it speaks to me about the faith of a little girl that knows that God sees and hears all that she does. Everything! Now that's a scary thought!

Psalm 139: 1-16 "O LORD, you have examined my heart
and know everything about me.
2 You know when I sit down or stand up.
You know my thoughts even when I'm far away.
3 You see me when I travel
and when I rest at home.
You know everything I do.
4 You know what I am going to say
even before I say it, LORD.

5 You go before me and follow me.
     You place your hand of blessing on my head.
6 Such knowledge is too wonderful for me,
     too great for me to understand!

7 I can never escape from your Spirit!
     I can never get away from your presence!
8 If I go up to heaven, you are there;
     if I go down to the grave, you are there.
9 If I ride the wings of the morning,
     if I dwell by the farthest oceans,
10 even there your hand will guide me,
     and your strength will support me.
11 I could ask the darkness to hide me
     and the light around me to become night—
 12 but even in darkness I cannot hide from you.
   To you the night shines as bright as day.
     Darkness and light are the same to you.

13 You made all the delicate, inner parts of my body
     and knit me together in my mother's womb.
14 Thank you for making me so wonderfully complex!
     Your workmanship is marvelous—how well I know it.
15 You watched me as I was being formed in utter seclusion,
     as I was woven together in the dark of the womb.
16 You saw me before I was born.
     Every day of my life was recorded in your book.
   Every moment was laid out
     before a single day had passed." (New Living Translation NLT)

God knows you inside and out, He saw you before you were born, watched you grow in the womb, knows every thought you will ever have, every act you will carry out on earth and the exact time when you will die. Yes, He knows you very well.

[God knows you inside and out]

For the little girl it was simply that she had been singing in a school show and it had been the highlight of her day, but she wanted God to be a part of the highlight of her day. What brings you the biggest pleasure in your life? Is God part of that? Would you want God to see you doing the thing that was the highlight of your day?

A few years ago the wristbands with WWJD were common and they were worn to highlight to others that the wearer was a Christian. They reminded the wearer that they were called to live as Jesus lived. So each day when faced with a situation they would ask "What would Jesus do?" So how do you live to please God?... You try to live each day as Jesus did.

 Teach

When we think about the things that make us smile and soar, do they involve God? We can play football, go shopping or deliver papers and still involve God.

Do you ever ask yourself, "what would Jesus do?"
When were you last sure that God liked what you had done?

The little girl was eager to please God and happy to talk about the everyday things in prayer. Wow! How many Christians do that? God loves it when we show faith, even simple faith in Him. Simple faith may be saying to God "I believe you are here, I believe you see everything, I believe you want to help me and be part of my life, guide me and I know that you will." To live out that prayer is to live in a way that will please God. Psalm 31:14-15 *"But I trust in you, O LORD; I say, "You are my God." My times are in your hands."*

May you live for God each day and truly experience His blessings as you do.

 Reach

> **God loves to see you happy!**

Everyone does things in life which will not please God – every day! You may be afraid that to be a Christian means stopping everything that does not involve reading the Bible, praying and singing (and wearing dodgy clothing!)

Does being a Christian and living to please God mean no more football, no more golf, no more music, no more parties or no more shopping? Absolutely not! God has created you to be like Him, which means you are designed to be social and enjoy time with others, to have fun and enjoy the benefits of creation.

1 Corinthians 10:23 *"You say, "I am allowed to do anything"—but not everything is good for you. You say, "I am allowed to do anything"—but not everything is beneficial."*

God loves to see you happy! There is one big proviso, except when what makes you happy, makes Him sad. When what makes you happy is not what God would want you to do, it's not what Jesus would do and it clearly goes against what the Bible commands you to do.

> **You need a childlike faith!**

To become a Christian needs a childlike faith. You need to simply admit the things that have been wrong in your life (not all of them one at a time as some of us would need a lot of time) then you have to trust that Jesus is God's Son and is able to forgive you and change you. 1 John 1:9 *"But if we confess our sins to God, He can always be trusted to forgive us and take our sins away."* (Contemporary English Version CEV)

God is interested in every area of your life and wants to be in your life but this only happens when we have faith in Him.

Are we nearly there yet?

Outline

To look at where the lives of the young people are heading? By looking at places we go, journeys that we take and looking at our ultimate destination.

Opening

There are few things worse than travelling with young children in a car on a long journey. The journey could be up to 3 hours but generally after just 15 minutes you hear "Are we nearly there yet?", "How long until we get there?", "I'm bored!" Parents definitely need a holiday after a journey like that! (Portable DVD players and MP3 players are a must for any journey over 1 hour!!)

So where do you like to go on holiday? Is it exotic, warm and sunny? Or is it somewhere in this country?

See if you can guess the places that I would like to go on holiday to, (*give 1 clue at a time and see how quickly they can guess*)

> It is always warm.
> It would take about 9 hours to fly there.
> Was an actor named after this City?
> It was made famous by a mouse.
> The theme park capital of the world. (Answer: Orlando)

> It is by the sea but you wouldn't want to swim in it!
> One of the most famous towns in the UK.
> It had a famous student at its University in the last 10 years.
> It is famous for being the oldest venue for a sport.
> The patron saint of Scotland. (Answer: St Andrews)

Everyone looks forward to going on holiday and it's great fun looking at the brochure or online to see what it will be like. However it isn't a great idea to believe all that you read in the brochure. For example it might say "only a 5 minute walk from the beach" which really means that if you can sprint like an Olympic athlete you might just do it in five minutes but if you are walking then it will be twenty minutes! Another one is "nicely situated in a quiet area with some shops and bars" which means that you are next door to the local disco that is bouncing until 3am and opposite a pub with karaoke competitions every night!

 Teach

So what about the biggest trip you will ever take? Eternity! The thing about eternity is that it lasts forever! So when you get there that's it, no coming back. The great thing about that thought for a Christian is that it is home.

John 14:2 *"In my Father's house are many rooms; if it were not so, I would have told you. I am going there to prepare a place for you."*

The Bible says that Jesus has gone to prepare a place for you to be with Him in heaven. Often at the end of a holiday you may be sad to come home and on some you have been glad to get back home but when you get to Heaven it will be the best place that you have ever been. There is a place in Heaven prepared especially for you! Your booking has been confirmed. Wow!

There is a place in Heaven prepared especially for you!

Let's look at how the Bible describes Heaven:
no pain, no suffering, no tears, no sin, no illness, no darkness, no fear, no favourites, no fighting. The Bible talks about light, streets paved with gold, joy, singing, meeting Jesus face to face! Unlike the travel brochure, this is one place that cannot be exaggerated, it's beyond words.

Are you excited about Heaven? You should be.

So if you are a Christian then why keep quiet? If you went to Orlando on holiday, you would tell everyone how good it was and or how much you are looking forward to it. You have a booking to the best place there will ever be, don't you want your friends to come too?

Matthew 28:19-20 says *"Go to the people of all nations and make them my disciples. Baptize them in the name of the Father, the Son, and the Holy Spirit, and teach them to do everything I have told you. I will be with you always, even until the end of the world."*

 Reach

This isn't a two week holiday we're talking about here, it's forever! Is everyone going to Heaven? How do you get there? It's very simple…you need a unique passport. 1 John 5:12 says *"He who has the Son has life; he who does not have the Son of God does not have life."*

The passport that God will look for is this; did you believe and trust in Jesus while you were on Earth? If the answer is "yes" then you have a booking in Heaven. If the answer is "no", then the Bible states that the only other destination is hell. This is a very difficult thought and one that is hard to explain. God is very clear that there is

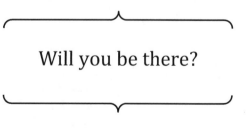

Will you be there?

no sin in Heaven so the only way that you can be in Heaven is if you have asked Him to forgive your sin. Revelation 21:27 *"Nothing impure will ever enter it, nor will anyone who does what is shameful or deceitful, but only those whose names are written in the Lamb's book of life."*

No-one can smuggle you in, there are no exemptions.

So amongst the places you decide to visit for a day or a week or 2 weeks on holiday this year, think about the decision you have to make that will determine where you spend eternity. The brochure (the Bible) which is more reliable than any holiday brochure says that Heaven is perfect!

Will you be there? Who will you ask to come with you?

What label are you wearing?

Outline

To look at the way that young people are influenced by things such as labels on clothing, football teams and music. What influence does peer pressure have on teenagers?

Opening

(Take along some items that would associate you with certain groups or teams)

I have brought a Liverpool hat, a small tie pin with my company logo and a Sherlock Holmes book. When I watch football I am never embarrassed to say that I support Liverpool or wear my top or scarf. They are my team and even when they get beaten I would still say that I support Liverpool. Then there is my tie pin, I'm not the "tie pin" kind of guy but I am not embarrassed of the company that I work for and am happy to wear my company badge or hand out my company business card. I belong to this company and they pay my wages so I am not ashamed of them. What about my Sherlock Holmes book? Well, when I go on holiday I sometimes take my illustrated Sherlock Holmes collection (yes it is a proper book) to relax and read on holiday (yes in public). I love the Sherlock Holmes stories, they are brilliant and I'm not embarrassed about reading them in public.

What are you embarrassed about? What do you like or not like to be associated with?

Teach

Baptism is a public declaration that you have decided to follow Jesus. At times you can be quiet about your faith and not particularly vocal about your "association" with Jesus. When you are baptised you are publicly stating that you are turning your back on your "old" life and choosing a new direction, which is to follow Jesus. It is a great feeling as you come out of the water and know that God is pleased at your public declaration of faith in Him.

> *the most important alliance in your life... He is yours and you are His.*

Why then do you struggle to be public about your faith? You don't hesitate to shout out which football team you "belong" to or which band is your favourite. But you hide away the most important alliance in your life which is that you have Jesus in your life. He is yours and you are His.

Be very careful Christians as the Bible says in Mark 8:38 *"Don't be ashamed of me and my message among these unfaithful and sinful people! If you are, the Son of Man will be ashamed of you when He comes in the glory of His Father with the holy angels."*(CEV)

Stand up and be counted!

 Reach

What is at the centre of your lives? What matters most? Is it being seen wearing the right labels? Is it being associated with the successful team of the moment? Chelsea or Rangers? Is it being part of the group that thinks they are cool by being drunk every Saturday night?

Who decides how you live? "I do", you cry. Really? Then what would happen if you chose to not go out on a Saturday night and not to drink or you chose not to pretend that your clothes are from Armani when they are really from Georgio (Asda!)

God demands that being a Christian means that He is at the centre of your life. That means nothing is more important than Him. It means that YOU choose to follow Him and ask Him to guide you each day; no one else chooses for you. You may be sitting there wondering if I am mad, I can almost hear you saying "have you met my friends? Do you know what they would say to me? I would have no friends…"

Trusting God is not just about eternity…..

Trusting God is not just about eternity, it's about trusting Him for today and believing that He is with you in every situation, no matter what your friends may say.

Matthew 19:26 *"Jesus looked at them and said, "With man this is impossible, but with God all things are possible.""* It's impossible for you to meet Sherlock Holmes, it looks impossible that Liverpool will ever win the Premiership. It is definitely impossible to please God and be in Heaven without having faith in Him.

Forget wearing the right labels, try wearing the badge that shows you trust in God every day (sometimes it might be hidden or squint) but without it you have no association with God.

What label is most important to you?

Glad tidings or grinch?

Outline

Do we appreciate the gifts we are given at Christmas? How often are we disappointed in them? How does this compare to our appreciation of God's gift of Jesus?

Opening

I love Christmas and get excited about it every year. I love the parties, the food, the presents, the presents…

On Christmas morning in our house we have some traditions (I think every house has them) we wake up early and meet in the upstairs hallway. We peek out of the window to see if it's a white Christmas, then slowly creep downstairs (in case Santa is still there). We are so excited and try to get a glimpse of the presents through the glass doors, but just as we are about to turn the handle and open the door, we stop and one of us says "we should really get the kids up!"

There are three presents that I have received that stand out for different reasons and all of them make me think about God's gift in a different way.

1. First is a present of a new golf club. The advert said that it hit the ball higher, further and straighter than any other club; I spotted this as I scanned the catalogues (as you do) prior to Christmas. So on Boxing Day I was desperate to try it out and arranged a game with 3 friends (to show off!) Sadly it all went wrong; the ball was going higher and further but in the wrong direction. I looked at the club wondering why it didn't work, thinking I'll take it back to the shop! The problem is of course me and not the club. It's my fault that the ball is going all over the place.

2. The second present was from my wife and it was a car. She had asked for a suggestion, so I suggested a fast, black car with sporty wheels. I was really excited but a bit worried as I had only bought her some perfume! Christmas morning came. Where had she hidden the car? Had she maybe just wrapped the keys? I did get the car, but was gutted! It was black, sporty, great looking wheels but was about a foot long and came with a remote control.

3. The third present is one that I receive every year, no not socks or chocolate. It is the Oor Wullie Annual (apologies to anyone outwith Scotland, it's like a Scottish Simpsons). Oor Wullie is great and I always look forward to getting it, normally at the bottom of my sack after I've opened all my big wrapped gifts. The problem is that I take it out of the bag and think ah I've got Oor Wullie again and throw it aside. I take it for granted.

Teach

What can we learn from these three gifts?

1. Unlike the driver, God's gift never failed. Jesus was exactly what you needed when you first became a Christian and is exactly what you need now. You may look back on this year and like my driver you may have gone a bit wayward. Jesus' offer of forgiveness remains consistent every day, every year.

2. What about the car? Do you judge how good your Christmas is by the expense of the gifts you receive? The most expensive gift you will ever get is the one you have already. God's gift of Jesus is beyond value, He is priceless.

3. What about Oor Wullie? Do you take Jesus for granted? I am a Christian you say, all is ok, I can wander away a bit and enjoy myself but God will forgive me. Yes He will but look back at the points above; God has given you the best gift, a perfect gift, a costly gift and one that can only confirm that you are loved. Now would you open a present in front of someone and say thanks I might use that someday and then throw it in the corner? No, then don't do it with Jesus.

"Thank God for his gift that is too wonderful for words!" 2 Corinthians 9:15 (CEV)

What an amazing gift Jesus was. It is so important that as Christians we remember what an amazing gift we have and that we enjoy this gift each day.

Reach

What does Christmas mean to you? Parties, presents, late nights, seeing friends, stuck at family get togethers, (don't worry even Christians try and avoid them!) So what about these presents?

1. The golf club is about the quest for perfection; you always want something better or newer and convince yourself that this is the answer. Be honest, it never is, or it only appears to be for a very short time. Jesus was God's Son who lived a perfect life and was the perfect gift as it brought us something we could never get ourselves – forgiveness.

2. The car is about cost. Everyone panics about spending enough on people at Christmas or at least as much as they will spend on you. So we all spend more than we should buying what we don't really need! (No I am not the Grinch) God chose to give you His Son so that you could be forgiven and have a personal relationship with Him. It's amazing when you think about it. The creator came to Earth and subjected Himself to death on a wooden cross in a most painful and costly way, to say I love you and want to forgive you.

3. The Oor Wullie annual is about throwing away a gift just because you are familiar with it. You might be thinking "yeah, yeah heard it all before", but hearing it and knowing it are totally different things. Please understand that just as the year will come when Oor Wullie will be missing from my sack of presents so it is true that one day God's gift will no longer be on offer. On that day you may have heard it before, but you will not be offered it again.

God's gift is not all wrapped in glossy paper with expensive bows. It is His Son, His gift to you that brings peace, forgiveness and joy. To receive it means saying thank you, acknowledging the perfect, expensive and most needed gift ever given. It's available to you now.

That's not fair God!

Just like Harry Enfield's character Kevin the stroppy teenager (*you may want to show a video from youtube*), we all at times cry out "That's not fair". Often it's directed at parents but it can be something that we say to God. So that begs the question, Is God fair?

Opening

> - You have just been blamed for something that you didn't do.
> - You have just been given into trouble for being late because you were told to go to the wrong room.
> - Your brother/sister has been allowed to do something that you weren't at their age.
> - You are being bullied at school or at home.
> - You feel like you are the one in the group who didn't get the good looks or the brilliant brains.
> - You have lost a family member or friend that you loved.
> - You are fighting an illness that won't seem to go away.
> - Your mum and dad have just split up and you are caught in the middle.
>
> Do you find yourself asking "why me God? Why does it always seem to be me? It is so unfair!"
>
> Life is hard at any age, problems and events in life are not restricted by age. We would all love life to be easy and for worries not to exist. Sadly until we get to Heaven that will not be the case. In Genesis where we read about how God created the world we learn that sin, death, illness, unhappiness all came about through one decision. God had created a perfect world and had given Adam and Eve free will over all that they had. Sadly they chose to do the one thing that God had forbidden. Just stop and think about that for one moment, they had the most beautiful world, living at peace with all animals and food aplenty, what more could they ask for?
>
> They wanted to be like God, they wanted to challenge the one instruction that He had given them. Was that fair? Can you imagine if you were given a Playstation3, Xbox, iPhone or new mountain bike for Christmas and you turned round and said "why didn't you get me a laptop?" Would that be fair? Or would you be ungrateful for all that you had received?

 **Teach**

Sometimes the things that we face in life are due to the fact we are Christians (persecution because of our faith), but often they are challenges faced by many people in life.

So how do we respond? Do we cry out "That's not fair!" or "Why me God?"

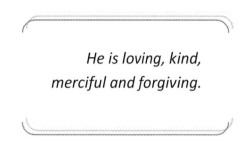

He is loving, kind, merciful and forgiving.

I know I have! But is it right to do this? Let's look at our God and His nature. He is loving, kind, merciful and forgiving. Is He by nature unfair? Well the Bible says that He does not treat us as our sins deserve. (Psalm 103:10) So if He was being fair and we got a fair reward for the lives we live then we would not be going to Heaven!

What about God's love? God created us and also let us have freewill to decide what we do with our lives. But knowing that we would sin and walk away from Him, He still chose to send Jesus into the world to die for you and I. Was that fair on Jesus? Was that deserved?

It is true that life can be hard and events can be very hard to understand but one factor overrides everything else…Gods love for us, His forgiveness and gift of eternal life are not deserved. Whatever happens in your life, remember that God cannot love us anymore than He does.

You have a wonderful assurance that God is with you, always.

 **Reach**

When you say life is not fair, who is that aimed at? Do you believe that all things that happen are random and unrelated? Is everything just a coincidence? You're either lucky or unlucky?

Let me be blunt. If you choose to ignore God, ignore what He wants in your life, refuse to acknowledge Him, don't accept that you need His forgiveness and don't believe that Jesus died for your sins, why would you think that it is fair that God welcomes you into Heaven when you die?

The truth is we often use the "It's not fair" in relation to things we don't understand. Lots of things have happened in my life that I won't understand until I get to Heaven and see the full picture. Therefore my trust is not in the fairness of life but in the fairness of God.

my trust is not in the fairness of life but in the fairness of God.

He has no favourites, He has no grudges, no vendettas; just simply a love that is available to all. He acknowledges that life will be tough at times and there will be tears. He also promises that if we trust in Him, that He will go ahead of us, be with us and carry us along the way. You can't say fairer than that, can you?

Are you happy?
Well do you want to tell your face?

 Outline

Why is it that people are sometimes happiest when they are miserable? Why is it that we chase happiness but never have any joy? Is there a difference? Does God want us to be happy?

 Opening

> Two prisoners standing in a cell
>
> They stare through the bars
>
> One only sees mud
>
> The other only stars
>
> (taken from a quote by Frederick Langbridge in A Cluster of Quiet Thoughts)
>
> Positive thinking, that's the key. Is the glass half empty or half full? Are you an optimist or a pessimist?
>
> We all love being happy, there is nothing wrong with being happy. Sadly there will be some Christians who give the impression that being a Christian and being happy are an impossible combination! What a sad truth that is!
>
> So it's ok to be happy? Yes. I am happy when I play golf (unless I play badly), I am happy when I play football (unless I get beaten), I am happy when I go on holiday, happy when I receive presents and happy to play with my family. All of these things are temporary, holidays pass, sports last for an hour or two, children start fighting. So happiness is fleeting. In many ways happiness is the nice things that come about in amongst the rest of life. That's why we notice it and like it when we feel happy because it stands out from the times when we don't feel as good about life.

Teach

"Rejoice in the Lord always." (Philippians 4:4) Not on good days, not because you won at football or because he fancies you too! No. Have joy in God **always**!

The overriding emotion in our Christian walk should be joy, so when the storm clouds of life come in we need to retain that joy. How?

"He that is in you is greater than he that is in the world."(1John 4:4) Regardless of what comes our way we are reminded that God is greater than it all, it sometimes doesn't feel that way, but it is true. Our joy is in the fact that God loves us, He cares for us and everywhere we go He is right there with us. Our joy is in the fact that our difficulties on earth are a passing storm compared to the blue sky and warmth of Heaven. That's not temporary, it doesn't last one hour, it is forever.

someone much bigger and better is in control of our lives and our destiny

Our ability to have joy does not depend on whether it is raining or the sun is shining, it doesn't depend on a good or bad day at school or work. It is a joy that knows that someone much bigger and better is in control of our lives and our destiny. That kind of joy brings a confidence that says "bring it on world because He who is in me is bigger than anything that you can throw at me!" That is faith, that is joy.

✝ Reach

Joy? What is joy? Is that like a girly name? Or a girly kind of happiness? You won't find many guys about to publicly say "I don't know about you, but I am feeling joyful today."

There will be many things that make you happy, most of them will be normal, healthy activities but often with happiness it is a case of needing to do more to have the same effect. So when you first got your PSP you were happy with 10 minutes of playing time but now you are grumpy if interrupted after 20 minutes because you haven't had enough yet. (It's called the law of diminishing returns, the more you do it, the less the effect)

This is true of alcohol, some young people experiment with alcohol and one drink makes them feel happy but after repeating this a few times they find that it takes three drinks to feel happy. What are we chasing? Is it a feeling of being ok, relaxed, under control, confident?

These things don't come from temporary happiness, they certainly don't come from alcohol or drugs. Our confidence, our feeling of relaxation, of being in control comes from a confidence in God.

He breaks this rule of diminishing returns; I get the same feeling out of my faith now than when I first became a Christian. I get the same

our joy is not temporary, it is eternal

feeling from reading the Bible for five minutes now as then, or praying. Why? Because our joy is not temporary, it is eternal. John 15:11 tells us that this is a joy that is complete so do you want to experience a joy, a love that never runs out?

Do you believe in stoning?

Outline

What are our priorities in life? How do we decide what is important? What if we are placing too much importance on the wrong things? What does God say is important?

Opening

If we go to school or work and have friends, family, hobbies, clubs and are involved in church then we will have lots of things that compete for our time. How do we decide what is the priority? What happens if we place all the emphasis on the things that are fun to do and avoid the things that are important? The answer is that we have fun for a short while but sooner or later the impact of not doing the important things hits us. It's a bit like wanting to go to University or get a good job but we constantly avoid studying because we like to watch MTV, play on the Xbox or be out with our friends. We may have fun in the short term but reality hits when we don't get the job or the place at Uni.

It's like having an empty bucket and we want to fill it with as many large stones, small stones, sand and water as possible. We start by seeing how many large stones will fit up to the top of the bucket, then the smaller stones fit in between the large stones. When we empty in the sand it finds the gaps that are left and finally the water still fills more space until the bucket is full. (Don't do this inside the house and don't try and lift the bucket!) If you try this in reverse you will get a lot less in the bucket as the water simply overflows. Why?

It makes sense to get the big things in first, just as it does in life. So what are the most important things in your life? There is a verse in the Bible that says *"Seek first the kingdom of God and His righteousness and all these things will be given to you as well"* (Matthew 6:33). What does that mean? God says give me my place – first place and the other things in life will find their proper place. If we have God as priority No.1 then we have the right perspective on our life. Often the bigger stones in life are more important but they take more effort so we avoid them. We like the easy things that fill the gaps like the sand or the water.

Teach

What are the stones in your life? What is the water? Are we avoiding putting God first? Do we try and fit Him in around everything else in our life? It doesn't work, we know that it doesn't work but what are we going to do to change it?

A man once asked Jesus what is the most important commandment and He replied *"Love the Lord your God with all your heart, soul and strength"* (Matthew 22:37), so here is our starting point. Do we love God with all of our heart, soul and strength? Is pleasing Him, serving Him and following Him the biggest stone in the bucket and the one that goes in first? If

> *Do we love God with all of our heart, soul and strength?*

not we need to empty the bucket. What do I mean, empty the bucket? Well, we need to go back to square one. Becoming a Christian involved a decision that God is real and a decision that we wanted God to be in our life and in charge of things…so put Him in first.

We don't always get things right but there is more chance of things being right and in their rightful place when God is in first! There are lots of examples of people who put God first, I think about Joseph who in the midst of difficult times (betrayed by family and left alone) and then very comfortable times (in charge of the whole country) always trusted God and put Him first regardless.

So what comes first, is it friends, popularity, hobbies, compromising so you can sit on the fence? There are many good things in all our lives but they only find their proper place once God has His.

✝ Reach

Do you ever think about what is important in life? Is that such a dull question that you think – give me a break I'm only 14! Ok so you don't have a wife and kids (I hope) but your life will revolve around certain things, school, friends, family, TV, music, alcohol, parties and more.

Some of the above are not really negotiable, you need to go to school five days a week and so you should. It's good to have friends and good to have hobbies. If you are like me then it's possible to have lots of things in life and be busy but sometimes not be happy. Why?

John 10:10 says *"I have come that you may have life and have it to the full."*

Jesus said that He came so that in Him we might have a quality of life that is otherwise not possible. That means without Him it is impossible to have the best life possible, which is quite a claim. We can have the best iPod, Xbox, clothes or shoes and still not have a life that is full. That's because the fullness is not full of stuff but rather full of love, peace, joy, fun and friendship that is not based on what we

> *without Him it is impossible to have the best life possible*

own but on what we have in Him. We don't believe that our faith gives us access to more money or more stuff but we firmly believe it gives us something that cannot be bought; fullness of life! Do you have it?

I will be back!

Jesus is coming to earth again! Why is it important to know that He is and does it make any difference?

Opening

There have been many heroes in British history and great adventurers over the centuries but have you heard of Ernest Shackleton? Shackleton was an explorer, an adventurer at the start of the 20th Century. In 1914 he captained the Endurance that left Plymouth on the 8th August 1914. The mission was to cross the Antarctic along with his crew. The plan was to sail as far as they could and then wait for the ice to freeze to enable them to traverse across the continent. However the ship was crushed in the ice and they were forced to abandon ship and try to retreat on foot, carrying all the supplies from the boat. They struggled and eventually made it to Elephant Island where they set up camp, 800 miles from the safety of South Georgia. Shackleton decided to leave twenty two men at the camp and travel with 5 men in an open lifeboat in treacherous seas to get help. The only way that navigator Frank Worsley could keep on track was via the stars and even then he only got a clear view of them five times during the voyage. On reaching South Georgia they were on the wrong side of a mountainous area that had never been crossed, Shackleton left three men with the lifeboat and took two men over the top and down into a whaling village to get the rescue started.

It is said that everyman on Elephant Island believed that Shackleton would return and day after day were prepared as though that was the day that the rescue would come. Wow! He must have been some leader, twenty two men wait on a island made of ice for 105 days, three men on rocks with a lifeboat trusting that their leader can do what no-one has ever done and then come back to get them. The great thing is that he did!

Teach

Are you ready? It is said that Shackleton's men packed their bags each morning in anticipation of their leaders return that day. Such was their belief in him they lived each day in expectation that he would come. Jesus has promised that He will come again. *"I have prepared a place for you and I will take you to be with me"* (John 14:2) It is a promise specifically for Christians; that place is in Heaven, made for you. Let's think for a minute about what the rescue meant, these men were starving, freezing, stranded and slowly dying. The rescue was everything. If their faith had been misplaced and their leader failed then they would never be found and would die. I wonder if people felt down and lost confidence during

71

those 105 days. I bet they did and some would have said "He is not coming back" or "He is dead, He never made it". Then some probably said "He said he would be back for us and to stay here so that's what we are going to do". How is your faith? Do you believe that Jesus will be back for you? Do you believe it could be today?

The answer to those questions will probably determine where you are in your Christian life because if you have lost sight of Jesus' return it will influence what you do. If I expected Jesus to come today I would be careful what I say, what I do and I would be living in a way that would please Him. Why? Because I would not want to meet Jesus when I was busy doing things that are not what He wants from me or to meet Him when I hadn't prayed or read the Bible in weeks? Months?

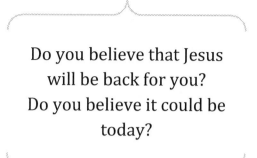

Do you believe that Jesus will be back for you? Do you believe it could be today?

I think that the hope and expectation that Shackleton was coming back kept those men alive, kept them focused and kept them together. When Christians forget that Jesus is coming back they lose hope, change what they do and how they behave. Is that you? Then think again that one far greater than Shackleton has promised to come back for you, the question is...are you ready?

✝ Reach

What do you place your hope in? Do you believe that this is it? You live, you die, the end. Do you believe that Jesus lived 2000 years ago? (History is full of evidence that He did.) So do you believe that He was a man, a prophet, the Son of God?

The men in Shackleton's boat were left on an island of ice floating on the freezing ocean. They knew it was a temporary home and that one way or another they could never stay there forever. God has said that He created the world but it is not designed to be our "home" forever. We will all die and then move on to another place forever. The Christian's hope is that through faith their home will be in Heaven either by death or if they are still alive, when Jesus returns. So what if you are not a Christian? The Bible is clear that Heaven is for those whose faith is in God, who have trusted in Jesus. If we don't know Him then Heaven will not be our home.

The Christian's hope is that through faith their home will be in Heaven

If some men had decided Shackleton was not coming back and wandered away on their own, they would have died and missed the rescue. Our world is crumbling through disease, war, crime, environmentally and socially. If we live in faith now then we will be rescued one way or another and spend forever in paradise. So do you want to be rescued?

Friends

Outline

To look at the example of Jesus as the ultimate friend and ask the question, what kind of friend am I?

Opening

Friends: one of the most watched programmes ever made, some of the highest paid TV actors in history, ten series, featuring six characters, New York, central perk coffee shop, every episode is called "The one about....", love, affairs, drama and friendship. Is that what you think friendship is all about? Is there anyone aged twelve or over who has not seen an episode of Friends? I know people with all ten series, the box set (with free poster). For some people the "veg TV" option is Friends on some channel showing endless repeats of episodes that they have seen twenty times before. Why?

Because it's comforting. Because it makes us feel good. Because deep down we wish we had friends like them. Friends that were faithful (ish), friends that we could laugh with, friends that never betrayed us, never left us, friends that were always there and we could always count on. There was Joey the daft but attractive one, Chandler the funny one, Ross the geeky but lovable one, Phoebe the wacky one, Rachel the attractive but ditzy one and Monica the once fat but now thin organizer. Something for everyone!

It's designed to make us feel good, make us laugh and make us wish that we were them. Whatever comes their way, their friends are there to see them through, always welcome in each others' houses and never in the way.

What about you? How are your friendships? Are you the one with all the friends that you want? Are you the one who feels on the outside of the group? Do you have one best friend or lots of people around you but no real close friend? The truth is that outside our family our friendships have the greatest capacity for fun, laughter and often, hurt. It has been said that we are a product of the six people we spend the most time with.

Teach

What are your friends like? What are you like as a friend? Big questions. What about this one, what does the Bible say about friendship? Or another, who is your best friend? Why have you chosen the friends that you have? Popularity? To be part of the cool crew? What does that mean for you?

Sadly friendship and the desire to fit in and be liked means that we sacrifice our values and do things that we should otherwise avoid. That can be in a park on Saturday night drinking with friends, it can be skipping school, using language that we would not normally use. Why? Scared to be different? In many ways we all are!

Jesus talks about a narrow road and a wide road in Matthew chapter 7. Christians are on the narrow road (not alone, just on the narrow road) so that means that we do not follow the crowd, we do not go with the flow. It does not mean that we don't have friends or don't get involved with the crowd – we just choose not to follow them.

He promises that His love is unconditional

Jesus' friendship is described in the Bible as being closer than a brother (Psalm 18:24). He promises never to leave us or turn His back on us; He promises that His love is unconditional. It's a friendship that is 24-7, it's supernatural. No bad moods, no huffs and no talking behind your back. So what is our friendship like with Him? Is He our best friend? Do we tell Him everything in prayer? Do we spend more time with him than anyone else? He wants to be the friend we value above all others, the one we turn to in good and bad times. Christian, don't hurt the friend who loves you more than any other. Some friends are there for a year or two but Jesus is here now and forever.

 Reach

Did you choose your friends or did they choose you? Maybe you think I sound really down on friends? Not at all! I have some very good friends, people I share private things with and trust them with issues that I need help with. That's a good thing to have. However we know that all of our friends have the ability to cause hurt and disappointment (just like us). At times they let us down, they make us feel second best or leave us out of things we want to be included in – at times we do exactly the same to them, we can all be selfish. There's one exception...Jesus. He offers a friendship that brings all that is good with no hidden motives.

He offers a friendship that brings all that is good

But of course it's not just friendship that He offers its friendship with a whole lot of extras. It's friendship where forgiveness is real not insincere, it's friendship with someone who never changes, friendship with someone who cares for you more than we do for Him. In this friendship you are never second best, never on the outside and never made to feel the odd one out.

They say we can choose our friends but we can't choose our family.

In Jesus you can choose your best friend and be part of God's family.

If you want my advice....

Outline

Who do young people look to for advice? They generally don't like receiving it but somewhere, somehow they follow someone's advice! But whose?

Opening

Have you ever been offered advice? Have you ever been offered advice you didn't ask for? Teenagers hate being given advice! Don't you? In truth we all do, when someone offers advice, it can appear that they believe we are incapable of getting decisions right on our own.

What's the best/worst advice you have been given?

- Never eat yellow snow (think about it!)
- Don't tie your laces in a swing door.
- If it's still moving, don't eat it.
- Check out your girlfriends mum because that's what she will look like in 30 years!
- Do your homework, it will be worth it in 10 years time.
- Any sentence that starts with "If I was you…" or "When I was young…"

We don't like it do we? Why? Is it because it implies that we have gotten it wrong or that we can't handle a situation? Sometimes when we get advice a small voice inside our head is yelling "How do you know? You are not me!"

Then sometimes we ask for advice and the person replies "Don't ask me!" or "That's really for you to decide!" Arghh! So you get advice when you don't want it but don't get it when you want it! Typical!

When we seek advice on a situation, it implies that we have a choice. Parents often enforce decisions, "you must" or "you will". In the Bible God spells out His advice for life. He gives us His commandments (Exodus Chapter 20) but it's our choice whether to follow them or not.

Teach

In my youth my pic'n'mix contained three different types of sweet, I would have five cola bottles, five white mice and five bonbons! This is not pic'n'mix! You can't decide to keep the commands in the Bible that are easy, non-offensive and are not done in public, keep the ones you like and forget the others.

Obedience is about believing that God is right. Believing that He knows the best way in every situation. To choose to obey in some ways and purposely disobey in others is like standing in front of God and telling Him "no I am sorry, you have got this one wrong! I believe you are right about being God, about being the creator, about forgiveness and Heaven. However when you talk about drunkenness or sex before marriage or needing to be baptized, I am not sure they are right."

If our trust is in a God that gets some things right and some wrong, then our faith is meaningless. For God to be God, He has to be perfect. He knows all things, sees all things, He is everywhere and He doesn't make mistakes. When I have a picture that this is my God I have a certainty that His advice is the best that I can get.

> *He knows all things, sees all things, He is everywhere and He doesn't make mistakes.*

 Reach

Who do you accept advice from? Is that because you believe that they know more than you? Is it because of the respect that you have for that person? What have they done to earn this position in your life? Normally we take advice from people that we admire, we respect or they have life experience.

Let me tell you a bit about God;

> He created the universe in 6 days,

> He knows the billions of people on the planet intimately,

> He says that He is the beginning and the end (He started everything and He will be here forever),

> He loves you and in the person of Jesus came to earth to show you His love,

> Jesus' life on earth was real. He experienced hunger, thirst, tears, laughter, friendship, betrayal, enemies and death.

> Why? For us. God came to earth knowing all that we would think, say and do.

Want advice? I would go to the person that made us, knows us better than anyone and knows what our future looks like. I would go to the person who has no other motive than wanting the best for us.

So what is His advice to us? *"Trust in the Lord with all of your heart, don't lean on your own understanding but in all your ways, acknowledge Him."* Proverbs 3:5.

If you want life, the best life, then follow Jesus. That's God's advice to you, are you going to take it?

Are you just going to leave me here?

Outline

To look at the subject of urgency in witnessing to our friends. Do we strive to make it a priority? What happens if we run out of time?

Opening

Imagine the scene (bear with me on this one as it's a bit Hollywood!), you are preparing for a big night out. It could be the football match of the year or the party of the year. Just as you are leaving you get a text to say that a friend of yours is tied to a railway track somewhere (told you it was a bit Hollywood but bear with me). You've been told where they are but you don't know when the next train is coming. It could be 30 minutes, 30 hours, 30 days. Is it a deserted train track so how much danger do you believe that they are in?

So here you are, preparing for the night of your life but now with a decision to make. In this scenario (like all good films) the phone lines are down and you don't have a signal on your mobile so you are the only one who can save them. What do you do?

Can you imagine not helping? Can you imagine leaving them there? If it happened in a film and the character went to the party or match you would say that would never happen!

Maybe not but then again in some ways maybe it does.

Teach

Let's forget the Hollywood storyline and look at the reality of this analogy. We are Christians, therefore we believe that we are forgiven and that through faith in Jesus we have been rescued from death and God's judgement. We believe that we will be in Heaven for eternity.

So let us consider our friends that are not Christians and who have not yet been rescued. So would we agree that they are in danger? Perhaps not in a physical sense as in the train track analogy but nevertheless in danger. As Christians we believe that Jesus will return to the earth to take Christians to be with Him in Heaven. Conversely we believe that those who are not Christians will not be in Heaven. So if tragedy was to strike (and sadly it does) then our friends who are not Christians would not be in Heaven.

So we have a responsibility then to tell them what we believe and why it is important for their life now and for eternity. How long have our friends been on that railway track?

How long will we leave them there? Perhaps you think that you are young and that your friends have years to make a decision about the Christian faith. Maybe you are right. But what happens if you are wrong?

> Statistics say that most people become Christians under the age of 17, so the longer you leave it the less likely your friend is to make that choice.

Does your faith make a difference to your life here and now? The Christian faith is about having the best life now, not just in Heaven. The best life for your friends is when they decide to follow Jesus, the best life for you is when you are obedient to your calling as a Christian. Part of our calling is to share our faith with others. It is a wonderful feeling to see friends that we have prayed for and spoken to about our faith become Christians.

Luke 15:6-7 says *"Then you will call in your friends and neighbours and say, "Let's celebrate! I've found my lost sheep."Jesus said, "In the same way there is more happiness in heaven because of one sinner who turns to God than over ninety-nine good people who don't need to."'"* (CEV)

Every person, every life, every decision made for God is significant.

So that leaves the killer question, do we really believe that they are in any danger? If you did, you wouldn't waste another day.

 Reach

Do you understand the analogy? Do you believe that there is any danger? Jesus talks about coming to seek and save the lost. In Luke chapter 15 Jesus tells a story about a lost sheep, one that is in danger and alone. The story is of a shepherd (Jesus) who goes looking for the lost sheep and carries it back to safety. This story illustrates Jesus' love for individuals and His willingness to rescue each one as if we were the only one in danger.

We would like to strike a balance in warning you about the danger of not believing without preaching Christianity through fear. The truth is that Jesus is the Saviour of the world, that's what we remember every Christmas! The baby called Jesus who came into the world, grew up and died aged thirty three on a cross.

For you it comes down to the question – what if Jesus has come to rescue you but you choose not to be rescued? What would life be like if you chose to be saved? What happens if you say "I don't want to be saved?"

> What if Jesus has come to rescue you but you choose not to be rescued?

Christians believe that the safest place that we can be is with God. What does that mean? To be forgiven, to have faith in Him and then to live life each day with faith that He is with us. To not live like that is to live in danger of God's judgement. Tough but true!

Questions, Questions

Outline

We all have questions in life, questions that we would ask God if we could. There are some questions we will never get the answer to and some that just don't have answers! But do you know the God who knows everything?

Opening

Children often ask the toughest questions, they definitely ask the funniest! I have a 6 year old son and here are some of his best ones:

Does God have a bed?
Will I have a bed in Heaven?
What does God look like?
Why did Jesus die?
How did God get to Heaven?
Does He have ladders?
Can God do magic?
How did God make grass?
Did God make all the houses?
Did God make the builders and they made the houses?
Did God make all people?
Did He mean to?
If Jesus is God's gift to us, did Santa bring Jesus?

Lots of us have questions about God and about life. Some questions involve things that we don't understand and some we will never understand. There are some questions that are nice to know the answer to and some that are important that we know the answer to.

Nice to know questions would be…
Where did God come from? What is Heaven like? Why do bad things happen to good people?

Important to know questions are…
What is God like? What does God want? What does God think of me? Why are we here? What happens when we die?

 **Teach**

Do we spend our time focusing on what we know or what we don't know? Think about the answers to the questions we have just thought about.

What is God like?
God is the almighty creator of the universe, He was here before anything else and He will be here forever. He is a God who loves all that He created.

What does God want?
God wants to have a relationship with each of us, He wants to forgive us and for us to live for Him.

What does God think of me?
God thinks we are wonderful and special. He knows all about us and therefore knows that we need His forgiveness. He knows what we could achieve if we trust and follow Him.

Why are we here?
We are here because God created us for His pleasure. After creating land, sea, stars, plants and animals, God still went on to create mankind and then said it was good.

What happens when we die?
When we die we will go to be in Heaven for eternity if we have put our faith in God.

● ● ●

take joy and strength in everything that you know already

● ● ●

As a Christian all those facts should be encouraging, amazing and build our faith in God. We believe in a God who knows all things and therefore we should trust that He knows best and although it can be hard to accept… we don't need to know all the answers. This doesn't mean that we should stop trying to find out more about our world, ourselves and God.

As you ask questions about what, why, how, when and where, remember to take joy and strength in everything that you know already and what you don't know, take comfort in the fact that God does know.

 **Reach**

What is it that you would like to know? My guess is that you would want some kind of proof that God is real. Some people ask why God does not show us that He is there and communicate with us. The answer is that **He has and He does**. Jesus was God in human form and lived for thirty three years on earth. God then inspired men to write the Bible so that we could have a constant communication from Him.

Some people question God's existence as they can't understand how a God of love can allow suffering, starvation and tragedies to occur each day. Those things, although sad, are predicted in the Bible where God tells us that He has given man freedom of choice but warns about abusing our freedom.

"It is absolutely clear that God has called you to a free life. Just make sure that you don't use this freedom as an excuse to do whatever you want to do and destroy your freedom. Rather, use your freedom to serve one another in love; that's how freedom grows. For everything we know about God's Word is summed up in a

single sentence: Love others as you love yourself. That's an act of true freedom. If you bite and ravage each other, watch out—in no time at all you will be annihilating each other, and where will your precious freedom be then?" (Galatians 5:13-15, The Message)

Does God want these things to happen? No. Does God allow them to happen? Yes.

As part of God's plan and creation you have freedom to choose what you think, what you say and what you do. These all have consequences but they all add up to make you the person that you are.

So here is a question for you…what if I am right and God created you, loves you and wants a relationship with you?
Here is another…what if you have it wrong?

The X Factor

Outline

To look at the most common and recognisable symbols in the world and what they mean to us. Do we recognize the significance of the cross?

Opening

You may wish to start with a selection of company logos on PowerPoint and get the group to guess the company.

A survey was carried out a few years ago that looked at the most recognised company logos in the world. Can you guess what the most widely recognised symbol was? Nike, BP, Ford….. No. Its McDonalds, the golden M is the symbol most people recognise and correctly associate with McDonalds. They have created a huge brand.

What is a brand? We are bombarded everyday with advertising on TV, radio, papers, magazines and billboards, all trying to get us to associate a name with a product and an image.

For example, if we played word association with Nike, what would you say?

Swoosh, Tiger Woods, Just do it, football strips, cool.

Nike have spent a fortune building the brand with adverts showing top sports stars wearing their clothing and using Nike equipment. The message they portray is that Nike is associated with success and the top sporting stars and if you buy Nike you will look and play like them. (If only!)

What about McDonalds? *(See how many items on the menu they can name)* It is the biggest fast food brand in the world. The Happy Meal, Big Mac and McFlurry are all household names.

What about the cross? What do we associate with the cross? For some it may be a piece of jewellery, a symbol of Christianity or something that is seen on church buildings.

If Nike tells us of sporting success and McDonalds' golden arches tell us of the world's most popular fast food, what does the cross tell us about Christianity?

 **Teach**

Do we appreciate the cross? Is it just another symbol in the world of logos and brands? Do we devalue it by putting it on jewellery, clothes and car stickers?

That may be a point for debate, but it is a fact that the Christian faith is centered around **the** cross of Jesus Christ. The cross speaks of God's love and sacrifice for mankind, the Christian faith is based on the belief that what occurred on that cross was of eternal significance.

It speaks of God's love reaching from Heaven to earth to touch your life and mine. Does that still impact your life day by day?

> *When the cross is central to our faith we remain centred in our faith.*

Companies sometimes change their logo or strapline to freshen up the brand but let's never devalue the cross by moving away from it or forgetting its importance. The cross is central to the Christian faith because of who died on it and why He died on it. When we lose sight of these things we lose sight of the person who is the centre of our faith. When the cross is central to our faith we remain centred in our faith.

 **Reach**

In Roman times there were thousands of people crucified as the roman army kept control of the countries they invaded. They would crucify those who committed crimes, those who opposed their rule and often to create fear in the area they controlled. Jesus was not the only man to be crucified, His was not the only cross.

So why the big deal about the cross then?

The Christian message is centered around the cross of Jesus. We believe that when Jesus died on the cross, He was dying not as punishment from the Romans but as punishment from God for OUR sins. We believe that Jesus died so that if we trust in Him then our sins would be forgiven. The cross is a symbol of Jesus stretching across the gap between man and God, the gap caused by our sin. Man alone could never bridge the gap, man could never be in God's presence otherwise as God is holy and we are far from holy!

> *The cross is a symbol of Jesus stretching across the gap between man and God, the gap caused by our sin.*

So the cross speaks of God reaching out to man and man being able to reach out to God through Jesus. Hebrews 12:2 says *"We must never stop looking to Jesus. He is the leader of our faith, and He is the one who makes our faith complete. He suffered death on a cross. But He accepted the shame of the cross as if it were nothing because of the joy He could see waiting for Him. And now He is sitting at the right side of God's throne."* (Easy to read version)

Yes there were thousands of crosses in New Testament times but none as important as the one that Jesus died on. Nike and McDonalds have big flashy brands but none will ever change the world in the way the cross of Jesus has. It wasn't about money, food or fashion but it was about life, death, forgiveness, love and eternity.

Next time you see a cross think about how it changed the world forever, then ask yourself if the cross of Jesus Christ has changed your life?

What do people say about you?

Outline

What impact does our life have on the people around us? How would they describe us? What are we known for? Does our life send out the right message to those we live with?

Opening

As we go through life people form opinions about us, some good, some not so good! Sometimes events in life can define the person and they become known for one thing. At the time of writing two people come to mind, Jade Goody and the pilot of the flight that landed in the Hudson River. The pilot will forever be known as the man who saved 155 lives by successfully landing a plane on the river after birds hit both engines (2009). That one event will ensure he is forever known as the hero of the Hudson!

Jade Goody is harder to summarise, she originally came to the fore in Big Brother as a lovable loudmouth. Then in Celebrity Big Brother she was involved in an infamous row with someone which resulted in racism allegations. Jade died from cancer within a few years of this scandal (2009). As the publicity of her illness had been so great many women have gone for tests and become aware of the benefits of testing for this disease. So after controversy and being disliked by many, her lasting legacy is in increasing the profile of her illness and in improving detection of this type of cancer.

In the Bible one of the disciples has been given a label over one incident that took place just after Jesus' death. Thomas was not present when Jesus appeared to the disciples and when he was told of Jesus' resurrection he famously said he won't believe unless he puts his fingers in the holes in Jesus' hands. Hence "doubting Thomas" is born and forever Thomas, one of the twelve disciples, will be known as the one who doubted.

However if we go back to John 11:16, we see a very different Thomas. Here he shows a courage and commitment to Jesus that shows a genuine faith. Thomas says he is prepared to travel with Jesus to Jerusalem (where Jesus has predicted His death) to die with Him!

Now that's faith! So why do we only remember the doubt?

 **Teach**

What's your reputation? Are you known as the caring, giving person to go to? Or are you the "no I don't do that" Christian? Or the one who is all theory and no practice? James tell us that faith is no good without action and that we need to live out our faith daily. (James 2:14-26)

The old adage is "don't just talk the talk but walk the walk". Make sure that you live out what you believe. Christians are often branded

> **Make sure that you live out what you believe!**

as hypocrites; people look at what we profess and then see us living out the opposite. It's impossible to be perfect – we are not – so we will make mistakes, say the wrong thing and do the wrong thing at times. It can be hard for people to understand that although we might say it's wrong to be greedy or lie or talk about others behind their backs, it doesn't mean that we will be immune to these faults ourselves.

However it is so important that we make every effort to live out our faith by showing love to those around us. Let's have the reputation of a joyful, loving, giving Christian because if others know us to have these qualities then its because they see us living out our faith in our actions.

Thomas was a doer, he wanted to **GO** with Jesus, **BE** alongside Him and then he wanted to physically **PUT** his hands on His risen Lord. Let's not be known as hypothetical Christians but as practical, real doers as well.

 **Reach**

What's your reputation? What sort of reputation do you want to have? Are you the hard man of the group? Are you the sporty one? The brainy one? Do you worry about your reputation or are you glad to be known for something?

Reputations are often easy to get and hard to lose. Thomas made a mistake 2000 years ago and he is still known for it. So if you like to be the girl who attracts lots of boys or the boy that likes to fight or is the daft one in class then beware, as this may be your reputation long after you leave school. God makes everyone with qualities and abilities that come in a combination that is unique to you. Isn't that amazing! But it's better to be known for what you are good at than to be notorious!

> **God loves you and is willing to forgive any mistake you have made**

Thomas is known as a doubter, a sceptic, someone who saw many miracles and witnessed Jesus first hand and then doubted his ability to rise from the dead. He lived, served and suffered alongside Jesus for three years but we only remember one thing. More importantly for Thomas though, was that God knew him as faithful!

"But if we confess our sins to God, he can always be trusted to forgive us and take our sins away."
(1 John 1:9 CEV)

Don't worry if you feel that one mistake has tainted you or will always be your reputation. God loves you and is willing to forgive **any** mistake you have made when you ask Him to. Thomas' life was more than one incident and your life is too. God can change reputations. He changed Paul's from a Christian killer to one of the New Testament's greatest Christians. Sometimes this is glossed over, Paul was on a mission to kill Christians and God purposely met him, forgave him, changed him and then used him to change the world.

He is still the same God and He has the same desire for you today as He had for Paul.

Our God is not into reputations, He is into new beginnings.

Great Expectations

Outline

To look at our expectations of the world around us, world leaders, teachers and parents and then look at how this compares to our expectations of God. We should also consider God's expectations of us.

Opening

As you came to this youth group tonight, what were your expectations? Did you think it would be good, better or rubbish? Has it lived up to your expectations?

In 2009 Barack Obama became President of the United States of America and the expectations the world had were massive. On this one man's shoulders were placed the huge issues of terrorism, financial crisis, racism and wars. Somehow the world had been sold the concept that Barack was superman and could turnaround several crises.

That's just not humanly possible!

What about you? What do people expect of you? Parents often place high expectations on exam results, they often want their children to outperform everyone academically. I can remember days when I had achieved a decent pass mark only to be asked "Who got the highest mark? How many people beat you?" My parents wanted me to be the best.

What were the expectations of Jesus when He first came to the publics attention? Some believed He was a rebel leader, someone to lead them against the Romans (a Zealot), some believed He would be a King to rival Caesar, some thought He was just a carpenter from Nazareth (and nothing good came out of Nazareth) and then there were those who believed that He was the Saviour and Messiah that had been predicted in the Old Testament.

- Your expectations of Jesus are based on who you believe Him to be.

- Regardless of whether you believe in Him, He believes in you and died for you.

- Does God have any expectations of us?

 Reach

Whether you believe in Him, the fact is He loves you and died for you.

What's your immediate response? "I don't care" or "I didn't ask Him to die for me" or "He doesn't even know me". Do you expect Jesus to love you and watch over you, even though you don't acknowledge Him? Probably not! But He does. The Bible tells us that we are loved as individuals, known by God even before we are born and that our every thought is known and noted by God. If God knows every bird in the sky, every blade of grass in the fields and every hair on your head then be assured that you are important to Him.

What does God desire from you?

A – acknowledge that Jesus is God's Son, the Saviour
B – believe that He died for you and took the punishment for your wrong thoughts, actions and words
C – confess your need of Him

God does not expect you to be perfect, He knows you are not. That is why you need Jesus.

 Teach

Sitting comfortably? You may be sitting thinking, "yes I have done that so I am ok". But what does God expect of us?

~ He expects us to live daily for Him. (Romans 12:1)
~ He expects us to serve in some way, maybe in the local church.
~ He expects us to tell others of our faith. (Matthew 28:19)

I wonder how comfortably you are sitting now? What about our expectations of God?

~ What do we expect of God each day?
~ Great things, small things… anything?
~ When was the last time that God was real to us?
~ When did we last involve God in our day?

God expects to be at the centre of our lives… is He?
He expects that you will speak to Him each day and trust Him for each day… do you?
Is our expectation of God too small, do we do it our way and miss out on great things?

> **Have great expectations of God!**

Ephesians 3:20 *"God can do anything, you know—far more than you could ever imagine or guess or request in your wildest dreams!"* (The Message)

What's your story?

 Outline

The Bible tells part of God's story but what story are we telling by the way we live?

Opening

I am always amazed by people who can read books but somehow the book never looks like it's been opened. Then there are others that turn the corner of the page down to mark the page every time they stop along with the coffee stains and dog eared cover!

We are all books that are read by the people around us, our words and actions are the story that we live out. From the moment that we are born until the day we die we write our story, day by day, hour by hour, the story of our life unfolds. Each day is a new page and different stages of life make up the different chapters.

When parents-to-be are expecting a new baby they often buy a book of baby names. Then they will choose a short list and think of the pros and cons of each name. Finally when the baby arrives they decide and the baby has a name.

God has a book of names, the Bible calls it the book of life, where the names of every person who has put their faith in Jesus is listed. This isn't a book where one name is picked out from the list like the baby's name but rather a book where it's essential that your name is on the list. The book of babies' names speaks of new life but the book of life speaks of eternal life.

Autobiographies are always interesting as they tell the story behind the person. In terms of sports men and women or actors they tell how they came from humble beginnings to become the star they are now. Then there is the disclosure of fallouts and relationships along the way that were previously unknown. Some are dull and boring – maybe the person is too young to have written an autobiography – some are incredible as they tell of exciting lives and great achievements.

So what's your story?

 **Teach**

What story is your life telling? Is it telling a story of two parts? The parts being before and after you became a Christian. Can your friends tell the difference between the two?

The book we haven't mentioned as yet is of course the Bible, where God tells us how He would like us to live our lives. He then allows us the freewill to choose how we live. Here is the amazing paradox of life: God allows you to choose what you do and say but He knows every moment of your life from beginning to end.

> **God allows you to choose what you do and say but He knows every moment of your life from beginning to end.**

So as Christians God expects us to live in such a way that others see Him in us, we are expected to live out our story in such a way that people see excitement, adventure and joy in us because of our faith. People were drawn to Jesus, they had never seen or heard anyone say or do the things that He did. He lived out the message and people found that compelling and even today the Bible is the world's bestselling book. Are people compelled to you because they see Jesus?

Are you reading the bible every day? How is your daily quiet time? Are the Bible notes under the bed or being used daily?

"The believers spent their time listening to the teaching of the apostles. They shared everything with each other. They ate together and prayed together." Acts 2:42 (Easy to Read Version)

It's so important that we read our Bibles and pray as this is where we learn from God and how we learn to write the story that God wants us to tell.

 **Reach**

The Bible can be the most intimidating book in the world, hundreds of pages long, full of "thou shalt nots" and where do you start?

First, what is the Bible about? It's a mixture of history, teaching and insight. The history refers to creation, the history of Israel and the early church (from Jesus birth until approx 98 AD). The teaching largely comes from the New Testament and Jesus' teaching to His disciples but also from letters written to the early church. Insight or prophesy would be parts of the Bible that tell of events that are yet to come, including how the world will end and what will happen when we die.

...when we follow Him we get the best possible journey through life.

The Bible tells us part of God's story from His desire to create to His desire for a relationship with us. Unless we know this and understand this we miss the main reason for our being. God has a plan (story) in mind for every individual and when we follow Him we get the best possible journey through life. At the end of our life God opens the book of our life and judges us accordingly.

So what story will your life tell? Will it be the one you were born to tell?

Will this stage of your life be the chapter where your name is written into the book of life?

The Church of Google

Who do we believe holds the answers to lives big questions? Some amazingly believe that Google is the source of all knowledge. There is even a church of Google! God says I am the beginning and the end. Before Google God was and after Google, God will still be!

Opening

Since the advent of the internet there has been a need to access the information on the net and of course the best known search engine is Google. It's amazing but some people ask Google the most bizarre questions in fact some of the most common questions are …..

Who do I look like? (How does Google know what you look like?)
Who do I think I look like? (worse than above!)
Who should I vote for? (people actually vote for someone based on the Google search)
Why do I fart so much? (depends on your definition of much!)
How do I kiss? (if you are asking your laptop then…..)
What is love?

So people rely on Google to give them guidance and wisdom for some big questions (and some not so big).

Then there is the "church of Google", which I can't quite decide if it's serious or not but they have 9 proofs that Google is God which are:

1. Google is the closest thing to an omniscient (all knowing) entity in existence, which can be scientifically verified (over 9.5 billion web pages) – *but when I googled me, I wasn't there!*

2. Google is everywhere at once (omnipresent) – *unless of course you don't have wifi/internet access.*

3. Google answers prayers, people search for things that concern them and find answers in Google.

4. Google is potentially immortal – *need I say more!*

5. Google is infinite – *so it is endless?… eh no… founded in the last 30 years)*

6. Google remembers all, once loaded information is never lost – *that's a joke, who hasn't lost stuff on a computer.*

7. Google can do no evil – *so you can't Google "how to make a bomb"?*

8. According to Google trends, Google is searched for more than God, Jesus, Allah or Buddha – *they believe this demonstrates that Google fulfills our need for God more than God does.*

So it begs the questions,

Who populates Google with information?
What has Google ever created that didn't already exist?
Is God just a collection of man intelligence or something far greater?

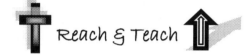

Reach & Teach

"Be still and know that I am God" (Psalm 46:10)   There is no other.

"Has not God made foolish the wisdom of the world?" (1Corinthians 1:20)

Google is fantastic, when I want to find a website, or a restaurant or new information I use Google. It's on my homepage and it works.

God is beyond fantastic. He created the universe by simply just speaking. He knows the stars individually (ask Google how many… then ask again in about 6 months time and the answer will change… scientists keep finding more). God knows exactly how many there are at any moment in time. God is capable of producing the hugeness of creation, yet knows the intimate thoughts of my mind, the hairs on my head and the seconds of my life.

When I come to the key crossroads of my life… What University should I go to?…What job should I do?… Who will I marry?… I will go to the God who knows everything and knows me inside out.

When I go into each day, I don't have to plug God in or switch Him on. He is right there with me, everywhere and all the time.

My trust is not in man or machine but in God my Saviour.

Where am I?

Outline

In life we are often searching for something but how do we find it? How do we know if we are looking for the "right" things? Are you searching for treasure or trash?

Opening

I was on holiday last year in Florida and like most people I visited the theme parks of Orlando. I remember being in the Magic Kingdom park and overhearing a conversation between a man and a member of staff.

> "Excuse me, can you tell me how to get to thunder mountain?"
> "Certainly Sir, it's in Adventureland, which lies just left of the castle" (lady points to thunder mountain on the map she is holding)
> "Thank you"
> "You're welcome"
> "Just one more thing, where am I now?"

It's a bit like getting a treasure map that shows mountains, rivers, forests and of course the place that marks the treasure but not really ever showing where you are or how to get there.

It's so frustrating knowing where you would like to be and wanting to get there, but the worst feeling is when you are lost and are having to ask "where am I"?

The Bible tells us -

- What we are
- Where we are
- Where we should be
- How to get there

What are you looking for in life? Happiness, good job, money, girlfriend/boyfriend, qualifications, fast car?

There is a verse in the Bible that says that where your heart is, this is where you treasure is also. (Matthew 6:21)

Another verse speaks of storing up treasures in Heaven where moths and decay cannot destroy them. (Matthew 6:19)

Teach

We have all been lost, sometimes in the car, sometimes in a strange town, sometimes in a supermarket (generally when you were under the age of 10!) It's not a nice feeling. Suddenly you feel scared, worried, isolated and you instinctively look for someone who can help.

Think back to the time when you first became a Christian or a time when you felt scared, alone and God seemed to be near and helped you back on track. Think of the contrast between feelings of being alone, scared and lost and then the opposite – feelings of comfort, calm, peace and safety in the arms of God.

It is a great thing to recall times of God's comfort and provision. As Moses led the people of Israel through the wilderness for forty years he had to cope with a group of grumbling people who thought they were lost. Moses constantly had to remind them of the God who had rescued them from Egypt, who had provided food from Heaven, water from a rock, protection from enemies and eventually the Promised Land. Was God lost? No. He knew exactly where they were heading.

So tell me how is your journey going? Are you grumbling? Have you lost your way? Who is holding the map?

> **When God is driving you will never be lost or alone.**

The reason that God should have the map and be in charge of your direction is because He knows the best way. It might not be the shortest route, the easiest route but it is the best route. So if you somehow feel that you have lost your way, ask yourself who is controlling the direction of your life?

As a Christian the destination is the same for us all, life is all about the journey. When God is driving you will never be lost or alone.

Reach

Can you remember ever being lost?

Do you feel lost at the moment? Luke chapter 15 tells the story of a lost sheep, there were 100 but only one was lost. The shepherd leaves the ninety nine and goes out to search for the lost sheep. I want you to think about a couple of really important points from this story.

- It's only the one who doesn't follow the shepherd that gets lost!
- It's the shepherd that goes looking for the sheep, not the other way about!

You were made to follow (some people won't enjoy that thought) but we all choose to follow something(s) – fashion, the crowd, a football team, God?

So the trouble comes for this sheep when it decides to stop following the person who keeps it safe, feeds it and cares for it. Incredibly it's the shepherd who decides not to simply abandon a wayward sheep but rather to risk danger and trouble by going after it.

The Bible says that if you don't believe that Jesus is your Saviour and God's Son then you are lost. Like the sheep you are wandering, but not where you should be. Like the sheep you are in greater danger when you don't stay with the one who looks after you.

> *Do you want to know what it feels like for Jesus to lead you and watch over you?*

Jesus said I have come to seek and save the lost. (Luke 19:10) That's you. If you don't know Him then you are living life without the right map and compass, your direction is all wrong. Jesus, like the shepherd has come looking for you; He faced danger and death to find you.

Today He looks across the field at you and asks do you want to be rescued? Do you want to know what it feels like for Jesus to lead you and watch over you?

Jesus is looking for you but only you can choose whether you want to be lost or found.

Telling your story

Outline

One of the most impactful things we can ever do is tell others "our story", the story of how we became a Christian and what God has done in our own life. So here is my story but I would encourage you to tell your own story.

Reach & Teach

I was brought up in a great home with loving parents and a younger sister. Like many children I was dragged to church in my childhood when I really wanted to be playing football with my friends! Whilst I didn't enjoy church services, I attended and loved Boys Brigade (BB) and Sunday school but lost interest when I went to secondary school.

At the age of about 14 I was part of a crowd that was involved in underage drinking and under 18 discos. It was the thing to do; hang about parks, drink two cans of lager and pretend to be drunk. At school I was underperforming and was the classic "could do better" school report! At this time a friend was asked to get a team together for a football competition being run by a local youth club. We played and won the competition on that dark and wet night. That was my first connection with Mark, with my church and the night I first saw my wife. We were invited to Bible class (youth group) on a Sunday afternoon and a few of us went occasionally. I look back now and recall that Mark would wait at the same point each week hoping that we would turn up so that he would give us a lift to church. (What an example of persistence and faithfulness that has been to me.) Out of the group of friends that went I was the one that enjoyed it most, probably due to my BB background.

At the start of my Higher/A-level year my friends changed to a more studious group and my school performance improved. I swapped hanging around parks for playing pool in a pals house on Saturday nights. On Fridays I still attended the youth club to play football and loved the chance to play every week. There was a five minute epilogue every week and this was never really an issue for me. Besides, there was also the girl that I fancied which was an added attraction!

I got through my exams and this started a period of great uncertainty; would I go to University or find a job? During this period I started to pray about my future and what I should do and asked God for His help and guidance. Although I cannot tell you a day or time, it was during this period that I prayed, asking God for His forgiveness and Jesus into my heart. It wasn't until September 13th that I knew what this meant. I usually sat through the announcements at Bible class (if I went) and never paid any attention as they were "church stuff". For some reason on Wednesday 13th September it occurred to me that something was happening that night at the church. I phoned Mark to ask what it was and he was amazed, his neighbour had just pulled out of a friends & neighbours dinner so he asked me to come along. I went with Mark and during the chat at the start of the meal I told him of my uncertainty and my prayers. He nearly fell off his seat and hardly touched his dinner! He confirmed that my prayer was my moment of becoming a Christian.

He encouraged me to go home and tell my family of my decision, which I did. I can still recall the evening where I walked to the houses of my closest pals to tell them of my decision and that I wouldn't be going on the boys' holiday that year. (The previous year had been one of late nights, too much alcohol, not enough food and half a stone of weight loss.) Telling my closest friends that I had become a Christian was one of the hardest and best things I have ever done. Within a month of becoming a Christian I asked the girl out (20 years later she is still here) and started University. I was a young Christian but had lots of old habits that wouldn't disappear quickly!

Six months later I was baptised and joined the church. A year later I started to help at the youth club that had been my first point of contact and eventually was the leader of the youth club for a number of years – standing giving the youth talks in the hall where I had sat that first night with the trophy!

A lot has changed since with jobs, marriage, children and youth leader roles. My faith has grown but my ability to get it wrong has sadly never gone! God has led my through some great times and some painful times. He has looked after me, blessed me and been very patient with me when I have been cold with Him.

I have had the joy of seeing young people become Christians, baptised, join the church, get married and start their own family. For a youth leader those are great moments when prayers are answered.

I give God thanks for the heart, the persistence and the prayers of the youth leaders at that time of my life. In my friend Mark who stopped his car to invite my friend to that football competition, who faithfully came to pick us up each week, who prayed for us and who took the time to build a relationship with me, I am reminded and challenged with the impact that one faithful Christian can have for God.